Tracing Your Family History

Rhonda R. McClure

pil Publications International, Ltd.

Rhonda R. McClure is a professional genealogist who began the search for her personal family tree 20 years ago. In her effort to learn more about her family and the best way to accomplish her research, she took courses through Brigham Young University and attended many genealogy conferences. Today she is a respected author and national lecturer guiding other newcomers through this exciting hobby.

Picture Credits:
Alamy Images: 22, 62; **Edelen/McGrier Family:** 9; **Sara Ewald:** 23, 31; **Julie L. Greene:** 25; **Anna Lender:** 12, 42; **Courtesy of the National Archives at College Park, MD:** 52; **Lucy Reynolds:** 11, **Matthew Scott:** 6, 24, 26; **Pamela Seatter:** 37; **Patricia Ulrich/Cynthia Sacks:** 7; **Ann Raffel Youngmann:** contents (center), 9, 43, 48.

Louis Weber, CEO
Publications International, Ltd.
7373 North Cicero Avenue
Lincolnwood, Illinois 60712

Permission is never granted for commercial purposes.

ISBN-13: 978-1-4127-1022-0
ISBN-10: 1-4127-1022-7

Manufactured in China.

8 7 6 5 4 3 2 1

CONTENTS

WHAT IS GENEALOGY?

Have you ever wanted to find out more about where you come from? Ever wondered why you look the way you do? Perhaps you have pondered why your great-grandparents came to the United States or how your family ended up in Australia. Or perhaps you just like solving puzzles or mysteries!

Researching your family history might be the biggest mystery of all. You may encounter great twists and turns as you begin to put together the pieces that make up your family tree. Each new find brings you to another generation, and with them come new things to search for and explain.

And that is what genealogy is: the researching of your family tree; learning about who came before you, and adding those names to a pedigree chart. Today this is more often referred to as *family history*, as you will quickly find that you want to learn more than just the names, dates, and places. Instead you will want to learn about the lives your ancestors lived. You'll find yourself on a quest for more

than just the nuts and bolts; chances are you'll yearn for information on what made them tick, what made them happy, and the trials they had to endure. The more you find out, the more you'll want to know—it's a never-ending puzzle. Family history is the hobby that continues to expand, because with each generation, the number of people you are tracing doubles.

Researching family history is an extremely popular hobby, now more than ever. There are many reasons for its increased popularity, but perhaps the biggest is the ever-growing use of the Internet. The Internet has changed the ways in which a family tree is researched, making it easier than ever. Records are now infinitely more accessible, research can be done at any time of day or night, and results are available at a much quicker pace.

When use of the Internet is combined with a more traditional search through records and repositories, researchers can discover loads of information about their families. The soulful images staring back at you from family pictures taken long ago will become true family members rather than just names on a sheet of paper.

It's All About You

Though family history is about those who came before you, the whole mystery actually begins with you. What you know about yourself and your immediate family is the starting point on the path to your pedigree.

Beginning with You

The first step to researching your family history is to think about yourself and what you already know. You know your birth date and where you were born. You probably have a copy of your birth certificate. If you have married, then you know when and where you were married. You already have the first pieces to your pedigree puzzle.

The reason you begin with yourself is because you are the individual from whom the tree traces back. You are the tip of the upside-down pyramid that you are about to build, and each generation adds twice as many people to the pyramid. There are

- 1 of you
- 2 of your parents
- 4 of your grandparents
- 8 of your great-grandparents
- 16 of your great-great-grandparents
- and so on!

As you identify any of the above, you immediately have two new questions to answer: Who is that person's mother? Who is their father? A pedigree chart (see page 6) is a great way to keep track of what you learn about each generation. The more you research, the more

I Was Born

When it comes to your own birth, you only know what you've been told about that day. Let's face it: You were a little young to remember the actual event. Your mother or father told you when and where you were born, and you may have photographs or a baby book lying around the house. But the information you have is all word of mouth; if you don't actually have a copy of your birth certificate to provide written documentation (for yourself and future generations), you should certainly obtain one.

The pedigree chart, also known as an ancestor chart, is the road map to your genealogy. At a glance you can tell what information you are lacking, either for an individual or for a generation.

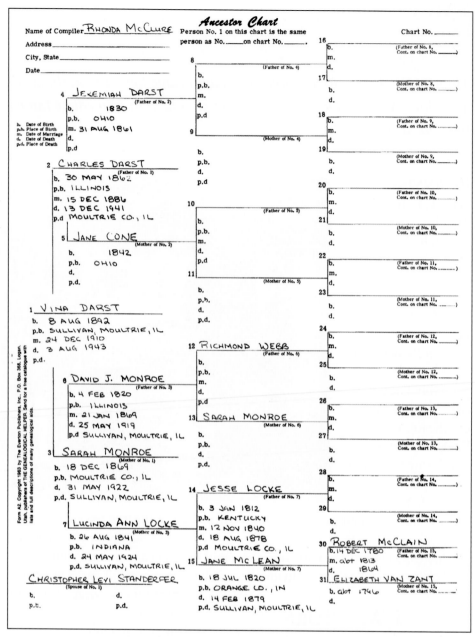

Ancestor Chart

Name of Compiler _RHONDA McCLURE_

Person No. 1 on this chart is the same person as No.____ on chart No.____.

Chart No. _____

Address _____

City, State _____

Date _____

b. Date of Birth
p.b. Place of Birth
m. Date of Marriage
d. Date of Death
p.d Place of Death

4 JEREMIAH DARST *(Father of No. 2)*
b. 1830
p.b. OHIO
m. 31 AUG 1861
d.
p.d

2 CHARLES DARST *(Father of No. 1)*
b. 30 MAY 1862
p.b. ILLINOIS
m. 15 DEC 1886
d. 13 DEC 1941
p.d MOULTRIE CO., IL

5 JANE CONE *(Mother of No. 2)*
b. 1842
p.b. OHIO
d.
p.d.

1 VINA DARST
b. 8 AUG 1892
p.b. SULLIVAN, MOULTRIE, IL
m. 24 DEC 1910
d. 3 AUG 1943
p.d.

6 DAVID J. MONROE *(Father of No. 3)*
b. 4 FEB 1820
p.b. ILLINOIS
m. 21 JAN 1869
d. 25 MAY 1919
p.d SULLIVAN, MOULTRIE, IL

3 SARAH MONROE *(Mother of No. 1)*
b. 18 DEC 1869
p.b. MOULTRIE CO., IL
d. 31 MAY 1922
p.d. SULLIVAN, MOULTRIE, IL

7 LUCINDA ANN LOCKE *(Mother of No. 3)*
b. 26 AUG 1841
p.b. INDIANA
d. 24 MAY 1924
p.d. SULLIVAN, MOULTRIE, IL

CHRISTOPHER LEVI STANDERFER *(Spouse of No. 1)*
b.   d.
p.b.   p.d.

8 *(Father of No. 4)*
b.
p.b.
m.
d.
p.d

9 *(Mother of No. 4)*
b.
p.b.
d.
p.d

10 *(Father of No. 5)*
b.
p.b.
m.
d.
p.d

11 *(Mother of No. 5)*
b.
p.b.
d.
p.d.

12 RICHMOND WEBB *(Father of No. 6)*
b.
p.b.
m.
d.
p.d

13 SARAH MONROE *(Mother of No. 6)*
b.
p.b.
d.
p.d.

14 JESSE LOCKE *(Father of No. 7)*
b. 3 JAN 1812
p.b. KENTUCKY
m. 12 NOV 1840
d. 18 AUG 1878
p.d MOULTRIE CO., IL

15 JANE McLEAN *(Mother of No. 7)*
b. 18 JUL 1820
p.b. ORANGE CO., IN
d. 14 FEB 1879
p.d. SULLIVAN, MOULTRIE, IL

16 *(Father of No. 8, Cont. on chart No.____)*
b.
m.
d.

17 *(Mother of No. 8, Cont. on chart No.____)*
b.
d.

18 *(Father of No. 9, Cont. on chart No.____)*
b.
m.
d.

19 *(Mother of No. 9, Cont. on chart No.____)*
b.
d.

20 *(Father of No. 10, Cont. on chart No.____)*
b.
m.
d.

21 *(Mother of No. 10, Cont. on chart No.____)*
b.
d.

22 *(Father of No. 11, Cont. on chart No.____)*
b.
m.
d.

23 *(Mother of No. 11, Cont. on chart No.____)*
b.
d.

24 *(Father of No. 12, Cont. on chart No.____)*
b.
m.
d.

25 *(Mother of No. 12, Cont. on chart No.____)*
b.
d.

26 *(Father of No. 13, Cont. on chart No.____)*
b.
m.
d.

27 *(Mother of No. 13, Cont. on chart No.____)*
b.
d.

28 *(Father of No. 14, Cont. on chart No.____)*
b.
m.
d.

29 *(Mother of No. 14, Cont. on chart No.____)*
b.
d.

30 ROBERT McCLAIN *(Father of No. 15, Cont. on chart No.____)*
b. 14 DEC 1780
m. abt 1813
d. 1864

31 ELIZABETH VAN ZANT *(Mother of No. 15, Cont. on chart No.____)*
b. abt 1746
d.

Form A2. Copyright 1983 by The Everton Publishers, Inc., P.O. Box 368, Logan, Utah, publishers of THE GENEALOGICAL HELPER. Send for a free catalogue with lists and full descriptions of many genealogical aids.

you'll realize how much there is to know about a given generation.

LOOKING BACK TO GO FORWARD

Because you are looking for the parents in each new generation, you might say that you are looking back to go forward on your pedigree. The more generations you trace, the further you have gone with your research.

While the pedigree chart is a good indication of the number of genera-

tions you have researched, the family group sheet is the story for each couple on your pedigree chart. (See page 10.)

Each couple in your direct lineage gave birth to at least one child; otherwise you wouldn't be here. The family group sheet allows you to record information about the children of each couple listed on the pedigree chart. Later in this chapter we will revisit the pedigree chart and family group sheet, but first we need to get back to you: You may

- What is your name?
- How old are you, and what is your birth date?
- Where were you born?
- Are you married, and for how long?
- When and where were you married?
- What are your parents' names?
- Where did you live when you were a child?
- Did you move around a lot as a child? Where?
- What were your parents' occupations?
- What is your occupation?
- Why did you pick that profession?
- Did your family get together often for holidays or special occasions? Who was there?

Once you answer these questions, you may be surprised to find out what you do know or, better yet, what you have remembered.

know a lot more about you and your family than you think you do.

THE SPOTLIGHT'S ON YOU

To delve into the story of your lineage, start by "interviewing" yourself. The answers to your own questions will launch you on your road to discovery.

When conducting these personal interviews, we often think to ask only the basic questions. Imagine you're in a courtroom being grilled: "Where were you on the night of the 21st?" Few of us remember such information without some kind of context.

Some of the following questions may make you feel as though you are grilling yourself, but they should help to spark memories—not only of yourself, but also of other family members. And that's the most useful information.

PUTTING THE SPOTLIGHT ON FAMILY

After you have asked and answered these questions, the next step is to ask similar questions of your family members. Interview your parents and siblings. It's a good idea to interview any older relatives as soon as possible. Too often people are left bemoaning the fact that they learned interesting details only after members of their family were no longer living.

If you find yourself in this situation, don't fret. While it makes the research difficult, be assured it *can*

Aunt Marie at the time? What else do they remember? By asking these kinds of questions, you may be able to jump-start the memories and obtain information your family didn't even know they knew. While they may not know Aunt Marie's exact date of birth, they may be able to tell you that she was 67 in 1977 when the big blizzard hit. And once they have remembered that, they may also remember something about where she came from. You now have something to work with! Remember, family history is a puzzle. Each piece adds to the big picture, and you'll find that there are lots of little pieces!

be accomplished. If you find there's no one in the family to ask questions of, look for old records. Paperwork can offer bits and pieces of information such as names, dates, and places. Don't despair if at first these are hard to come by: As you delve deeper into your research, you'll discover a number of resources.

When interviewing family members, don't simply interrogate them. Instead of asking them to tell you what they know about Aunt Marie, ask them to tell you about a particular family gathering. How old was

GETTING IT ON PAPER: WRITING DOWN WHAT YOU KNOW

At this early stage, you might think you'll remember everything you find out. But it's not a good idea to rely on your memory. You'll be surprised at how quickly the facts fade and blur together. Was Great-Grandpa Charlie born in New York or Philadelphia? Did Grandma Rose have one sister or two? It is best to write down the facts as soon as you learn them. Each memory, each event, even family stories, need to be written down so you can decipher them and retrieve the pertinent details.

There is no "right" way to record your information; it is simply

LEADING QUESTIONS

Don't limit your questions to those that give you names, dates, and places. Instead, ask questions that may lead the interviewee to open up and share feelings or special memories. For example:
  • What is your favorite color?
  • What is your most vivid childhood memory? Why?
  • What is your favorite movie?
  • What is your favorite book?
  • How did you ask your spouse to marry you?
  Questions such as these may help you discover insight into the whole person, giving you a better understanding of your family history in the end.

important that you do. You may decide to use loose-leaf notebook paper and a three-ring binder. The following is one approach you might take: Divide your notebook into two sections. In the first, record names, dates, and places of events for particular people. In the second, record stories or answers to interview questions.

Section 1: Write the name of the person at the top of the page; in parentheses indicate their relationship to you as best you can. For instance, if you know John Smith as your cousin, don't worry about what kind of cousin he is. Having the relationship prominently displayed will prove helpful later so you won't have to flip through your research trying to recall who the person is. It's best to organize these pages alphabetically by last name.

Section 2: Record the name of the person or resource from whom you got the information. Be sure to include the date you got the infor-

mation and how you came by it. Was it a letter? Did you actually chat with that person? Next, put the address of the individual. It is a good idea to include as much information as you have: e-mail addresses, mailing addresses, phone numbers. This provides many avenues for contacting that individual later if necessary. On the rest of the page, record the information itself.

You are beginning to build your case. You are getting details about your family that will lead to the next step: getting records and verifying the information you have learned.

FAMILY GROUP SHEETS

As you obtain information about your siblings or your parents' siblings, you'll find that there is no place on the pedigree chart to record this information. The family group sheet goes hand-in-hand with the pedigree chart; it is where you'll record information you learn about siblings.

Don't be worried if you don't have exact dates of birth or marriage as you write information on the family group sheet. The family group sheet helps you think in terms of family groups: the father, mother, and children. Each couple on your pedigree chart is a family group. It's likely you'll need to research the

PENCIL IT IN

Always use a pencil when writing on a pedigree chart or a family group sheet. This allows you to go back later and add or change information if you discover new answers.

Q. What is a direct ancestor? Is it different from an ancestor in general?

Your ancestor is someone from whom you descend. Many people use the term "direct ancestor" to identify a direct lineage from that person to you, and the term "ancestor" to indicate everyone in that family unit. But you can use either term.

siblings of your direct ancestors in order to go back another generation.

NAMES, DATES, AND PLACES

By now you may have figured out that researching your family history means dealing with a lot of names, dates, and places. Stories provide a more complete picture of your ancestors, but at first the nuts and bolts are the most important aspects of genealogy.

Genealogy is a hobby, and like many hobbies, there are certain guidelines that should be followed.

In genealogy, the major guidelines involve how to record the names, dates, and places you uncover.

What's in a Name?

There's a lot in a name, actually. For starters, names usually consist of a first and last name. Many individuals also have a middle name. And many married women have a maiden name. In family history the first and middle names are known as *given names,* and the last name is known as the *surname.* We spend a lot of time concentrating on the

Family group sheets provide a more detailed look at the whole family unit, rather than just information about the parents, as found in the pedigree chart.

Family Group Sheet

Husband's Full Name ROBERT McCLAIN   **Chart No.**

Husband's Data	Day Month Year	City, Town or Place	County or Province, etc.	State or Country	Add. Info. on Husband
Birth	14 DEC 1780			PENNSYLVANIA	
Chr'nd					
Marr.	abt 1813				
Death	1864		ORANGE CO.	INDIANA	
Burial					

Places of Residence

Occupation   Church Affiliation   Military Rec.

Other wives if any. No. (1) etc.
Make separate sheet for each marr.

His Father DANIEL McCLAIN   Mother's Maiden Name NANCY

Wife's Full Maiden Name ELIZABETH VAN ZANT

Wife's Data	Day Month Year	City, Town or Place	County or Province, etc.	State or Country	Add. Info. on Wife
Birth	abt 1796			KENTUCKY	
Chr'nd					
Death					
Burial					

Places of Residence

Occupation   Church Affiliation   Military Rec.

Other husbands if any. No. (1) (2) etc.
Make separate sheet for each marr.

Her Father   Mother's Maiden Name

Sex	Children's Names in Full (Arrange in order of birth)	Children's Data	Day Month Year	City, Town or Place	County or Province, etc.	State or Country	Add. info. on Children
M	1 WILLIAM McCLAIN	Birth	1814			KENTUCKY	
		Marr.	10 MAR 1834		ORANGE CO.	INDIANA	
	Full Name of Spouse MARTHA IRVINE	Death	1 SEP 1870		ORANGE CO.	INDIANA	
		Burial					
M	2 JOHN McCLAIN	Birth	1818			INDIANA	
		Marr.	bef 1845				
	Full Name of Spouse CHARLOTTE J.	Death					
		Burial					
F	3 JANE McCLAIN	Birth	18 JUL 1820		ORANGE CO.	INDIANA	
		Marr.	12 NOV 1840		ORANGE CO.	INDIANA	
	Full Name of Spouse JESSE LOCKE	Death	14 FEB 1879	SULLIVAN	MOULTRIE CO.	ILLINOIS	
		Burial					
F	4 MARGARET McCLAIN	Birth	1825			INDIANA	
		Marr.	18 AUG 1848		ORANGE CO.	INDIANA	
	Full Name of Spouse WILLIAM G. BAKER	Death	27 JUL 1894		ORANGE CO.	INDIANA	
		Burial					
F	5 ELIZA McCLAIN	Birth	1828			INDIANA	
		Marr.					
	Full Name of Spouse	Death					
		Burial					
F	6 EMILY McCLAIN	Birth	25 SEP 1830			INDIANA	
		Marr.	4 JAN 1844		ORANGE CO.	INDIANA	
	Full Name of Spouse WILLIAM CHISHAM	Death	8 JUN 1860		ORANGE CO.	INDIANA	
		Burial					
F	7 SARAH ANN McCLAIN	Birth	abt 1833			INDIANA	
		Marr.	23 OCT 1851		ORANGE CO.	INDIANA	
	Full Name of Spouse WALTER MOODY	Death					
		Burial					
M	8 ISAIAH McCLAIN	Birth	25 FEB 1839			INDIANA	
		Marr.					
	Full Name of Spouse	Death	17 NOV 1875		ORANGE CO.	INDIANA	
		Burial					

Compiler   Notes:

Address

City, State, Zip

Date

(left margin of form) From #160 Family Group Sheet by The Everton Publishers, P.O. Box 368, Logan, UT 84321. Publishers of The Genealogical Helper. Send for a free catalogue within and full description of many genealogical aids.

(vertical label) Husband's Full Name

surname. After all, if you have your father's surname, you probably share *his* father's surname as well, because it is likely that he has his father's surname. While there are exceptions to this rule (as there are to all others), the most common way to begin your search is to focus on surnames. You should note that in genealogy, because the surname is so important, women are listed by their maiden name.

Middle names may provide hidden clues: Don't ignore them. In some cultures, it is not uncommon for the maiden name of the mother to be handed down as a middle name to one or more of her children so that the name is remembered. Other times the middle name is significant because it has ties to a surname found in earlier generations.

When writing the names on forms (always using pencil!), identify the surname by writing it in capital letters. This is especially important when the surname has more than one word in it. Surnames such as *DE LA*

VERGNE or *ST. CROIX* need to be written in all caps so that other researchers can distinguish the surname from the given name. Remember, surnames are what you spend a great deal of time looking for, so knowing just what that surname is becomes even more important.

Perhaps one of the biggest mistakes new family historians make is to presume that a person is not related if the surname is spelled differently. Spelling, especially as it pertains to names, is a contemporary issue, gaining momentum in the mid–1900s.

It is not uncommon to find the name of an individual of a previous era spelled different ways throughout his life. Sometimes you may even discover that the name is spelled two or more ways within the same record.

Spelling variations are also the result of a clerk or enumerator's interpretation of the name. This is especially true of ethnic names—eastern European names with silent consonants, for instance—that sound quite different than they were actually spelled. As a result, genealogists have to be somewhat creative when it comes to identifying potential spelling variations.

What do I do if I don't know a woman's maiden name?

This is a common problem, especially as your research takes you back to the 1800s. Most women took the name of their husband, and their maiden name is often missing from records from then on. If you are unable to find a marriage record, you are left with just a given name for a woman. That is how you should record her until you can identify her maiden name. Never use another surname, such as her husband's, to identify her. It's better to show just her given name, because that lets you know the information you are missing.

THE *PATRONYMICS* EXCEPTION

One major exception to the surname rule is found in ethnic groups that use *patronymics*. Patronymics is a naming system in which a child takes his father's given name as part of his surname. For instance, if Pietre is the son of Johan Jorgeson, instead of being named Pietre Jorgeson, he would be known as Pietre Johanson. Patronymics may be found in Scandinavian, Icelandic, Dutch, Welsh, Slavic, and some Russian families.

Q. It would be so much quicker to record dates in this way: 3/6/32. Why can't I do that?

A. Dates written with just numbers can be misinterpreted. In America, that date would be read as March 6, 1932. In Europe, the same date would be interpreted as June 3, 1932. And, of course, since the year is recorded with only two digits, there is a great deal of assumption when it comes to the actual year.

Handwriting plays a role in variant spellings as well, especially when you use an index that was compiled a long time after the original record was created. The people who created many of the indexes we now rely on, such as census indexes, had to make sense of the sometimes hard-to-decipher writing of the 1700s and 1800s. It may be easier for you, a family member on a mission, to recognize the surname of your ancestor within the handwritten record, than the indexer, who looked at the same census page and had to decipher a surname from the jumble of letters on the page.

Got a Date?

When recording dates in your family history, follow a few helpful guidelines designed to allow you to communicate with fellow family historians around the world. If you follow these simple rules, others won't have to guess when they read the information you share. By the same token, you won't have to guess about information you receive from others if they follow the same guidelines.

- **Years are always listed with all four digits.** The first dates you will begin seeking are probably from events that occurred in the 1900s, but eventually you will trace the family back to the

1800s—and even earlier. Obviously, it is important to identify those centuries whenever you record a date.

- **Spell out at least the first three letters of each month.** When it comes to genealogical practices, leave no uncertainty. You don't want people to wonder which part of the date is the month and which part is the day. So, when you record dates in your forms or notebook pages, write them in the following style: *18 Jun 1756.*

He Was from Where?

If someone told you your ancestor was from Bloomington, would you think he was from Indiana? Illinois? Kansas? It might surprise you to discover that there are 22 cities and towns in the United States named Bloomington—in 20 states. (Yep, two states—Kansas and Pennsylvania—have two cities each named Bloomington.)

So just how does one indicate which Bloomington is the correct one? In family history, this is done

---

TRY YOUR HAND AT IT

To anticipate possible variations of surnames, try writing the surname in script in different ways, some of them neat and tidy, others scrawled and messy. Make other samples as ornate as possible. Then look at those samples and try to see which letters might be misread or misinterpreted. This should help you imagine variant spellings that might lead you to your ancestors.

---

by listing the complete place name, beginning with the smallest jurisdiction. If your ancestor was born in Bloomington, Indiana, record the place as *Bloomington, Monroe County, Indiana*. Listing places this way leaves no question as to where someone was born.

It is also important to record the country of origin. Even though your immediate family may have spent their entire lives in the country where you currently live, it is likely that at some point they or their ancestors came from another country. As you advance in your genealogy, you may correspond with other genealogists in other countries. Identifying full place names will eliminate miscommunication.

GRANDMA SAID WHAT?

Perhaps you are familiar with the game Telephone, in which a group of people sits in a circle and one person whispers a message in their neighbor's ear. The message is passed around the circle from person to person, and at the end of the game the last person says aloud what they heard. In almost every game, the ending statement is completely different from the original.

Family traditions and stories can be a lot like that game. The more they are told, the less they may resemble the original story. However, among the embellishments, there are almost always grains of truth. Your job is to ferret out those truths. But in order to do that, you must first know the story.

Listen carefully when someone begins a story. Or, if you remember a story you once heard, ask a relative to tell it again. Write down what they tell you, or if they will let you, record them with a tape recorder or video camera. Even though these days a tape recorder is considered old-fashioned compared to a video camera, sometimes it is a better tool. It is less obtrusive, fading into the background and allowing people to forget they are being recorded at all. A video camera is quite visible and may inhibit the person sharing the story. Use whichever works best for you; there's no set rule.

After recording, transcribe the interview. Next, make a few copies of the transcription. Leave one untouched, and use the other copies in your research, highlighting facts and making notes on the transcription. Notes would include those facts you have been able (or unable) to verify, as well as those for which you have leads. Eventually you will separate truths from embellishments. You might find out that while your great-great-grandfather did not ride with Jesse James, as you had always heard, he did live in the town where Jesse James once resided.

TAKING THE NEXT STEP

Up to this point we have talked about getting facts from your memory and the memories of others in the family. The next step is to look around your house and collect all the papers you can find, such as

Q. How do I record the town where my great-grandmother was born if it no longer exists?

A. When recording events about your ancestors, always list the place name as it existed at the time the event took place. Towns get incorporated into larger cities over time. Newer counties split off from older counties as the population begins to grow. However, the records that you seek are usually found in the county or town where the event took place.

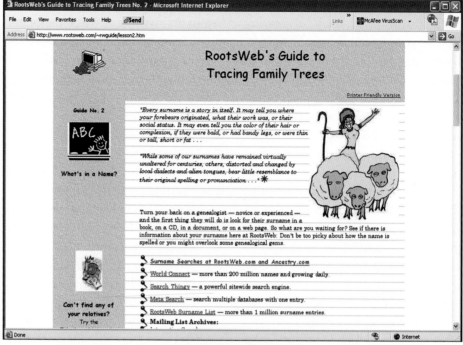

birth certificates, marriage certificates, and family letters. Once you have them all together, begin to go through them systematically. It's a good idea to make photocopies of each so that you can mark them up as you did the transcripts of the family stories. Circle or highlight information such as name, date of birth or age, place of birth, date of death or burial, place of death or burial, and any information about marriage, including the date, place, and who married the couple.

When you are looking at letters, treat them the same way you would the family stories. Look for information about travels, news of births or birthdays, descriptions of parties to celebrate anniversaries, or talk of visits to a family gravesite. Sadly, letter writing is becoming a lost art in today's world of instant e-mail, and yet for genealogists, yesterday's letters are treasure troves of information that may even spark fond memories for you.

MOVING OUTSIDE THE HOUSE

In genealogy, one must work from the known to the unknown. This is done by obtaining records and other items that help you verify what you know. In these records, family histories, and other resources, you will also find tidbits about individuals you knew nothing about.

So now it's time to ask your family members to share any papers they have. Tread lightly until you know how your relatives will react to your new interest in family history. Some family members may be less than enthusiastic and may not leap at the chance to share items in their possession, while others will be more than happy to share papers, mementos, photographs, diaries, and more. When contacting any relative about their personal papers, make it clear that you will pay to have them copied. That way they

A GOOD INTRODUCTION

For an introduction to many of the different records you may need, visit RootsWeb's Guide to Tracing Family Trees (rwguide.rootsweb.com). This site contains all sorts of tutorials on topics ranging from ethnic and religious research to how to use city directories and newspapers more thoroughly. The lessons include links to other sites that contain more helpful information or, in some cases, actual data.

won't worry that you are never going to return them. If they don't live too far away, consider paying them a visit during which you can ask to tape-record them as you both look through photographs or diaries and letters.

When it comes to family members who are not forthcoming, give it some time. They may come around as you share discoveries of family origin, trials they survived, or perhaps even famous relations. Eventually they may let down their guard and share the mementos they have.

GOING BEYOND THE FAMILY

Eventually you will exhaust all the records in your or your family's possession. You will then need to request records from courthouses and state vital statistics agencies. Request a copy of your own birth certificate and marriage license if you don't already have them. In addition to verifying that you were indeed born when and where you thought you were, your birth certificate will tell you the ages of your parents at the time of your birth. Some will also tell you where your parents were born. You may already know all of this, but consider getting these certificates as practice for later.

Obtaining a copy of your own birth certificate is easy: You are legally entitled to it. As you work on other family members' histories, however, you may find that the state has restrictions on entitlement to birth or death records, while the county courthouse does not. Also, you may discover that the state's records don't go back far enough. Most states did not require vital records until the 1900s; however, individual counties often recorded

SAVE YOURSELF SOME TIME

You could spend hours trying to identify the courthouse or state agency from which to request copies of birth, marriage, or death certificates, as well as records for the time period that you need. So, genealogists rely on *Ancestry's Red Book: American State, County, & Town Sources,* 3rd edition, by Alice Eichholz. The charts in this book are the result of questionnaires and additional research that determined the records of each county courthouse, as well as the addresses to use to contact them. Information for each state also includes the address for the state vital records office as well as the requirements for access to the records.

You may also find the courthouse or state agency you need at PublicRecordSources.com (www.publicrecordsources.com). They have a subscription site that supplies detailed information about the state and county repositories, as well as a free area that lists those state and county sites that are available on the Web for free. For instance, the "Free Public Record Sites" link will take you to a list of the states and other links. Here you can find out how to request records, download required forms, and learn more about what these repositories offer.

marriages when the county was founded and shortly thereafter began recording births and deaths. Finally, try not to get discouraged if you discover that neither the state nor the county has the record that you want. You soon will be introduced to other records that may supply you with the information you seek.

Most states now have special forms that you need to submit with an accompanying fee when requesting vital records. Many states have made such forms available on the Internet. You simply need to print them out, fill them in, and send them off.

RESEARCH LOGS

Family historians use a number of different resources in their quest. Research logs are essential tools for keeping it all straight so you don't

Q. A photocopy of a picture is not going to look nearly as good as the original. Is there any way to get a good duplicate without having to send the photographs off in the mail?

A. Copy centers usually have high-quality scanners that can create a duplicate photograph. You can choose to print it, put it on a computer disk, or both.

A PLACE FOR NOTHING, AND NOTHING IN ITS PLACE

Don't forget to record in your log the sources that turned up nothing as well as those that provided information. A research log plays an especially important role for those instances in which you think you've reached a dead end. You may forget that you found nothing and accidentally return to that source.

duplicate your work later. Even if you don't see the need for a research log during the beginning stages, it's a good bet that eventually you will forget some of the early records you searched. You can prevent this by indicating important facts in a research log, such as:

- where the search was conducted (library, archives, family papers, etc.)
- when the search was conducted (be sure to list the full date, including the year)
- the record or other research used
- the information you did or did not find.

You can create a log on paper, of course, but many people feel it is easier and more convenient to create and maintain it with a word processing program. Use the table function in any word processing program to create the initial table; the sizes of the rows will self-adjust based on the amount of information in each cell of the table. You can be as specific in your information as necessary, giving as many details as you'd like.

MORE THAN VITAL RECORDS

As you progress in your research, you will find that there are many different types of records that are useful in supplying pieces to your pedigree puzzle. You may want to use our resources checklist or create your own to track the record types you use.

RESOURCES CHECKLIST

Keeping a checklist for each couple on your pedigree chart will help you remember where you are in that

A log in progress. Notice how the information cites library call numbers, lists full source information, and gives detailed comments about what was or wasn't found.

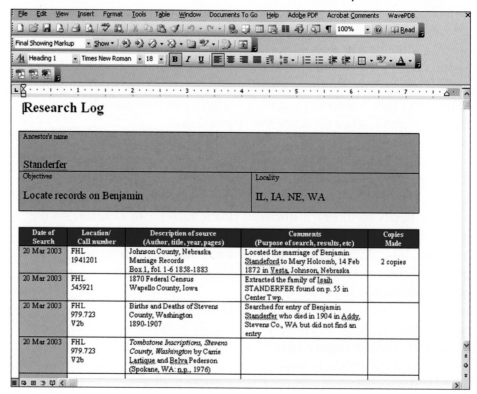

SAMPLE RESOURCES CHECKLIST

HUSBAND'S NAME
James Eads

WIFE'S MAIDEN NAME
Martha Winston

Vital Records
Birth (H) _b. ca. 1792, no record exists_
Birth (W) _b. 12 Mar 1801, baptism record_
Marriage (H) _m. 9 Jun 1821 – marr. rec._
Marriage (W) _____ see above
Death (H) _d. 23 Aug 1868, tombstone_
Death (W) _d. 1840, tombstone_

US Federal Census Records
1790 (H) _____ N/A
1790 (W) _____ N/A
1800 (H) _George Eads, 1800 NC_
1800 (W) _____ N/A
1810 (H) _George Eads, 1810 NC_
1810 (W) _James Winston, 1810 NC_
1820 (H) _James Eads, 1820 NC_
1820 (W) _James Winston, 1820 NC_
1830 (H) _James Eads, 1830 NC_
1830 (W) _____ see above
1840 (H) _James Eads, 1840 NC_
1840 (W) _____ see above
1850 (H) _James Eads, 1850 NC_
1850 (W) _____ N/A
1860 (H) _James Eads, 1860 NC_
1860 (W) _____ N/A
1870 (H) _____
1870 (W) _____

1880 (H) _____
1880 (W) _____
1880 Soundex (H)[___] (W)[___]
1890 (H) _____
1890 (W) _____
1900 (H) _____
1900 (W) _____
1900 Soundex (H)[___] (W)[___]
1910 (H) _____
1910 (W) _____
1910 Miracode (H)[___] (W)[___]
1920 (H) _____
1920 (W) _____
1920 Soundex (H)[___] (W)[___]
1930 (H) _____
1930 (W) _____

State Census Records
(H) _non-existent for time period_
(W) _non-existent for time period_

Mortality Schedules
(H) _____ N/A
(W) _____ N/A

Probate Records
Will (H) _died intestate (no will)_
Will (W) _____ N/A
Inventories (H) _Surry Co., NC courthouse_
Inventories (W) _____ N/A
Settlement of estates (H) _Surry Co., NC courthouse_

research. When combined with the research log, a resources checklist lets you track your results as well as the records you have yet to check. Keep in mind that not all the categories listed on the checklist are appropriate in every search given the years of birth and death of each couple. Some of the records may not have existed. Perhaps you know there was no divorce between two individuals, so you have not checked those records. A sample resources checklist for a project in progress is shown above.

Many of these records may seem foreign to you when you start out. As you read further and take those first steps in genealogy, you will be introduced to some of them. For a detailed list of the information you may find in these records, see the table on page 50.

Checklists and research logs are great, but you may find that a good genealogy program can track these items and much more for you, making it easier to know where you are in your research. Computers have simplified much of what genealogists do, allowing more time for the actual thrill of the hunt. Remember, family history is a hobby, and you should be having fun with it. Read on!

COMPUTERS AND YOUR FAMILY HISTORY

Genealogy software is the first step in computerizing your family history. Changes are more easily made with software, and the variety of reports, charts, and forms provided ensures that there is something to suit your needs.

WHY USE A GENEALOGY PROGRAM?

Genealogy software has been around since the 1980s. Since those early programs came out, a lot has changed in genealogy—particularly the methods we use to research and share our ancestry with others. Genealogy programs have kept up with these changes and with the advances in computer technology in general. These programs are valuable time-savers.

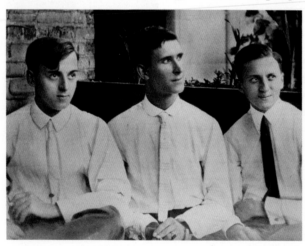

The best genealogy programs help you cut down on duplication. When using forms such as pedigree charts and family history sheets to organize your ancestors into family units, you'll find yourself recording the same information in more than one place. In the pedigree chart you'll list name, date and place of birth, date and place of marriage, and date and place of death. Then you'll record the same information on one or more family group sheets. That's a lot of writing! If you use a genealogy program, however, you enter the information once and then direct the software application to incorporate that data into whichever form you want.

Is that Information Correct?

A good genealogy program has a lot more to offer than simply saving you some time. What are the benefits? A good genealogy program will

- Alert you if you enter conflicting information. Say you enter "1845" as the year of birth and then accidentally key in "1809" rather than "1908" for the date of death. The program will catch the mistake and notify you so you can fix it right away.
- Let you enter information only once. You can then recall that information from *lists*. Once you type in a place name, such as *Haverhill, Essex County, Massachusetts*, for example, you'll never have to type it again. The program allows you to select that place instead of retyping it.
- Help you with consistency. Reducing the number of times you type something reduces the potential for typos or omission of information.
- Give you a place to store notes and family stories.
- Help you create a family history book, with pictures of family members or documents.
- Give you the tools to create your own Web page so you can share your research with family members all over the globe.

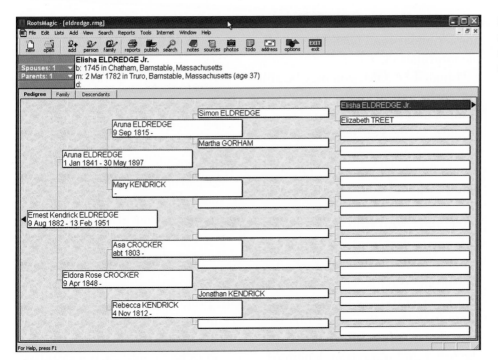

Elisha ELDREDGE Jr.
b: 1745 in Chatham, Barnstable, Massachusetts
m: 2 Mar 1782 in Truro, Barnstable, Massachusetts (age 37)
d:

Pedigree | Family | Descendants

- Elisha ELDREDGE Jr.
- Elizabeth TREET
- Simon ELDREDGE
- Aruna ELDREDGE 9 Sep 1815 -
- Martha GORHAM
- Aruna ELDREDGE 1 Jan 1841 - 30 May 1897
- Mary KENDRICK -
- Ernest Kendrick ELDREDGE 9 Aug 1882 - 13 Feb 1951
- Asa CROCKER abt 1803 -
- Eldora Rose CROCKER 9 Apr 1848 -
- Jonathan KENDRICK
- Rebecca KENDRICK 4 Nov 1812 -

Programs like RootsMagic eliminate much of the duplication genealogists endured before computers.

NOT ALL PROGRAMS ARE CREATED EQUAL

As you research genealogy programs, other things to consider are ease of use, the number of events in a person's life you can record, the cost, and the provision of technical support for the program.

Another important feature to many people is the *interface*. The interface is what the screens look like as you are entering information about your ancestors. If you find the fields of the program confusing, or find it difficult to locate menu items, it's a safe bet you will be frustrated with the program. And that defeats its purpose! It would be smart to find a different program.

As a beginning genealogist, you may not have an idea what you want in a program. After all, you are a beginner and don't yet know all that you will want to record about an ancestor. As you travel deeper into your family history, you may find that the genealogy program you started with doesn't do everything you require now.

What is GEDCOM?

The acronym GEDCOM stands for GEnealogy Data COMmunication. This feature, which is built into genealogy programs, allows users to create a file in which the information from one genealogy program can be exported and transferred into another program. Sometimes the transfer of data goes smoothly, but other times you may have to clean

Is there a correct way to cite sources in genealogy?

Q.A.

A source citation should be clear enough so that a total stranger can use it to get to the place you found the information. When citing a birth certificate, you should include the name of the child, the certificate number, the year of birth, the state or county office from which you requested it, and the town and state in which that office is located. Census record citations should include the name of the individual found in the census, the year of the census, complete place location, page and district numbers, and microfilm information for the census film used. Each source, whether book, vital record, census, or tombstone, requires different information in the citation. It is always better to cite too much than not enough information so there are no questions as to where you got the name, date, place, event, or story.

up the file because the new program doesn't understand where to put all the information.

Using GEDCOM, you may be able to transfer your data from one program to another with minimal cleanup, saving yourself hours of retyping. Your genealogy program should be a help, not a hindrance. Don't stick with it if it frustrates you.

Try Before You Buy

Before you decide on a genealogy program, you may want to see which ones offer a demo version that lets you try it out before you commit. A few offer only a predefined demo; others allow you to use the program for a certain length of time or up to a certain number of people researched. Two programs, Personal Ancestral File (PAF) and Legacy, are free. However, the free version of Legacy advertises all sorts of extras that you must purchase.

Trying before you buy is the best way to know if you will like a spe-

cific program or interface. If it seems intuitive to you—that is, you just know where all the options are going to be found—then it's probably a good program for you.

SOURCE CITATION

Good genealogists cite their sources. A source is any record, letter, interview, or other resource that has supplied you with the information you've recorded. Sources include

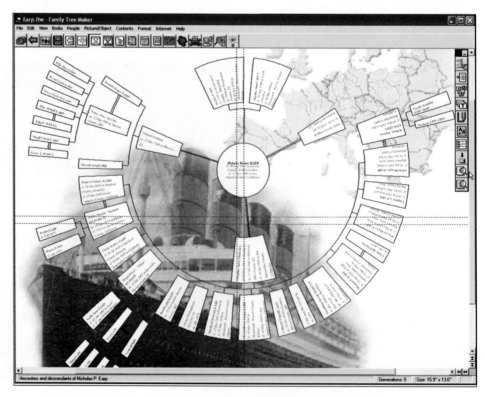

Genealogy programs such as Family Tree Maker offer creative ways to display your family tree.

vital records, wills, tombstones, baptism certificates, letters, Web sites, and anything else used in the research process. Anytime you add a name, date, place, or relationship to your genealogy database or to your family group sheets and pedigree charts, make sure you have a source connected to it.

All genealogy programs include at least one template for creating a source list; there are a few programs that offer many different templates. It's important to remember where you found your information. You never know when you'll want to go back and confirm a fact, especially if subsequent research doesn't match

GENEALOGY SOFTWARE PACKAGES

Name	Contact Information	Web Site Address	Operating System
Ancestral Quest	Incline Software, LC P.O. Box 95543 South Jordan, UT 84095-0543	http://www.ancquest.com/	Windows 3.1, Windows 95, or higher
Brother's Keeper	Brother's Keeper 6907 Childsdale Ave. Rockford, MI 49341 FAX 616-866-3345	http://www.bkwin.org/	Windows 3.1, Windows 95, or higher
Cumberland Family Tree	Cumberland Family Software 385 Idaho Springs Road Clarksville, TN 37043	http://www.cf-software.com/	Windows 95 or higher
Family Matters	MatterWare 3522 Sandy Ridge Trail DeLand, FL 32724	http://www.matterware.com/	Windows 3.1, Windows 95, or higher
Family Tree Maker	MyFamily.com, Inc. 360 W. 4800 N. Provo, UT 84604	http://www.genealogy.com/	Windows 95 or higher
Legacy	Millennia Corporation P.O. Box 1800 Duvall, WA 98019	http://www.legacyfamilytree.com/	Windows 95 or higher
Personal Ancestral File	The Church of Jesus Christ of Latter-day Saints	http://www.familysearch.org/	Windows 95 or higher
Reunion	Leister Productions P.O. Box 289 Mechanicsburg, PA 17055	http://www.leisterpro.com/	Macintosh
RootsMagic	RootsMagic, Inc. P.O. Box 495 Springville, UT 84663	http://www.rootsmagic.com/	Windows 95 or higher
The Master Genealogist	Wholly Genes, Inc. 5144 Flowertuft Court Columbia, MD 21044	http://www.whollygenes.com/	Windows 95 or higher

Why has a church created a genealogy program?

The Church of Jesus Christ of Latter-day Saints, whose congregants are more commonly known as Mormons, has a special place in their beliefs for genealogy. They believe that families can be together forever, but that they must first be identified and then "sealed" together through special temple ordinances. To this end, the Church has one of the largest genealogy libraries, and it is open to anyone. You will learn more about their library in chapter 5, From the Internet to the Library... and Beyond.

what you have listed, or if someone asks where you found the information. So, to save yourself time and grief in the long run, take the time now to create a comprehensive record of source citations.

MAKING YOUR COMPUTER WORK FOR YOU

When genealogy programs first came out, most researchers were used to using pedigree charts, family group sheets, or even index cards to

track their family histories. Technology has come a long way since then, but some genealogists haven't yet embraced all the different ways that computers can be used in genealogical research. Organizing your ancestors into family units is one of the only ways in which computers are helpful. There are a number of software applications created with genealogists in mind that can expedite your search in other ways.

Obviously the presence of the Internet is extraordinarily useful. You'll learn more about that in chapter 3, Heading onto the Internet. For now, let's look at some other software applications for organizing or evaluating the facts you uncover.

Organizing Data

While genealogy database programs organize the individuals in your family tree, there are other programs to help you organize the facts you uncover as you progress in your research. Some of them are specialty programs, whereas others are programs you may be familiar with already, such as word processing programs and spreadsheet applications.

Programs such as Clooz (www.clooz.com) offer templates of some of the more frequently used record types. These templates allow you to abstract specific facts when making a photocopy of the record is not possible. The benefit of such a program is that you don't have to remember the important points to abstract. It's a great way to ensure that you get the pertinent information from the record—especially for people just beginning their research, who might not know exactly what to look for. Clooz also allows you to look at the information in a different

ABSTRACT VS. TRANSCRIBE

There are two terms heard frequently in genealogy when it comes to the information found in a given record. The first is *abstract,* which indicates that the researcher selected pertinent details from the record to either enter into a computer or write on a form or piece of paper. The second, *transcribe,* indicates that the researcher copied the entire record verbatim, right down to the misspelled words. Both have their purposes in genealogy. Abstracts are good for documents such as birth, death, or marriage certificates. Transcriptions should be reserved for any record subject to misinterpretation, or for records that offer more information than an abstract would accommodate. Also, certain letters might be better transcribed than abstracted in order to show the personality of the writer as well as the facts.

way: Instead of combining people into a family unit, which is what a genealogy database program does, these applications *remove* the family connections. People are linked only through records. This change in focus provides a different way to view the information and often reveals relationships you had previously overlooked.

WHAT ELSE CAN A COMPUTER DO?

There is no limit to how your computer can help you track your family history. Be creative and demand a lot from your genealogy programs and your computer. You can

- Abstract information found in cemeteries or census records.
- Diagram pieces of land based on descriptions found in land deeds.
- Track medical information.
- Create elaborate charts or use timelines to aid you in your research.

WHERE TO TURN FOR HELP

When it comes to genealogy programs, there are a number of places to go for assistance. First, there is

the help option built into the program as well as the accompanying printed manual. There are also books that focus on specific genealogy programs, some of them written by genealogists for genealogists, some of them written by the developer or programmer. To find what is available for the program you are using, try visiting bookstore Web sites, such as Amazon.com, and entering the name of your genealogy program to see what comes up.

Mailing lists and bulletin boards on the Internet are another good resource. (See chapter 4.) Sometimes the program's developer monitors these communication avenues, but most of the best help comes from other genealogists.

HEADING ONTO THE INTERNET

The convenience of the Internet has changed how genealogists research their family tree. Most now check the Internet first—before looking for traditional records and repositories. Genealogy has become one of the most popular subjects on the Internet.

How trustworthy is the information on the Internet?

The genealogy found on the Internet comes from many different sources and many genealogists with varying degrees of experience. As such, there is always the potential for error. Information found on most of the Web pages used by genealogists would be categorized as "secondary" research; that is, data compiled by someone who was not present at the time of the event. Such research always needs to be verified.

UNDERSTANDING WHAT THE INTERNET OFFERS

Over the past decade or so, there has been a major shift in how genealogy is researched. Before there was such a thing as the Internet, everything had to be done on site, through visits to libraries, archives, and courthouses. Today a lot of the preliminary research can be done from the comfort of your own home at your convenience. Consider the Internet a library that is open 24 hours a day, 7 days a week, 365 days a year. This library that never closes is now the first stop when it comes to family history.

WHAT YOU NEED TO KNOW BEFORE YOU START

To find ancestors from recent generations, you may need only a few basic facts to start searching online. When looking for information on earlier generations, however, it's best if you have a little more knowledge before you begin. It's a good idea to keep the information you know beside your computer, easily accessible in case you need it. If you have entered data into any of the genealogy programs discussed in chapter 2, use the report feature in the program to print out your pedigree chart and appropriate family group sheets. Having your notes close at hand makes it possible to

quickly check what you already know, or suspect, as you search for information online. As you visit various sites, keep in mind that negative results, especially this early in your research, do not automatically mean you've hit a dead end. You may need to go back and ask family members a few more questions before you are able to make any headway online.

Remember that the Internet contains information about everything: There are times when searching for a specific name may lead you to a site that has nothing to do with your research. This is usually an issue only when using *general search engines* (see page 27). However, when you travel to family history sites, you may discover that your name is a lot more common than you originally suspected.

As you search for your family on the Internet, try to use as many hard facts as you can. Searching for just a surname may quickly bring frustration. Many people share the same surname without sharing the same ancestry.

KEEPING PACE WITH YOUR RESEARCH

Keep track of the sites you visit and the information you do or do not find. Research logs are the best way to do this (see pages 15–16). The research log templates created over the years were designed primarily for traditional research with books and documents; however, they are also useful for research done on the Internet.

Be sure to record every site you visit. When surfing the Web, it's easy to lose track of the sites you visit as you click one link after another. Three hours later, you may not remember how you got to some of them. Some sites will yield useful information; some will be a bust. Still others may not contain any-

thing directly relevant but will lead you to a more useful site. Recording even those sites that yielded no information will save you a second fruitless visit in the future.

Don't forget to list the names you were looking for when you conducted the research. Why? Because ten years from now the only aid you will have to refresh your memory is the tips you include in the research log or in the notes of your genealogy program.

Whenever you find information about your family online, print it out immediately. The Internet is an ever-changing entity. Often when you try to return to a site, it has vanished. Printing a hard copy is a guarantee that you can refer to the information at a later date. Even better, if you return to that site you'll be able to compare the current information on the site with the pages you printed out previously. If you find that any data has changed, you can make note of it on your printout or, if there are extensive changes, print a new version and file both of them.

A SOURCE SUBJECT

As you venture onto the Internet, look for source citations. In a compiled family history, look for super-scripted numbers after dates, places, or sentences. Check to see that the

Q. What is negative research, and how is it tracked?

A. Negative research is the term used to refer to those records and resources that do *not* reveal information about your ancestors. The problem with tracking negative research is that often it produces no tangible records—unlike positive research, which yields photocopies or notes.

DROWNING IN A SEA OF PAPERWORK

In the beginning it's no big deal to keep track of the few notes and documents you find in the house or the letters you receive from cousins or other relatives. But eventually you'll need a way to track the pages you print from the Internet and the many copies you acquire from other resources. There is no one method that's best for everyone; what matters is that it works for *you*. No matter what type of system you come up with, it's a good idea to set it up sooner rather than later!

Web page compiler has supplied the identifying information about a source. For instance, if the site is devoted to the records of a specific cemetery, did they:

- include the name of the cemetery?
- identify where the cemetery is located (address or town)?
- include the date they walked the cemetery abstracting the tombstone data?
- tell you who abstracted the data?

These facts help you to know how complete the information is. If the cemetery was originally walked in 1967, it's possible that some tombstones included in the Web site's pages no longer exist. By the same token, it's possible that the information was not taken from the cemetery itself, but from papers created in 1967. If this is the case, you have to consider the possibility that errors were introduced when it was uploaded to the computer.

Remember that the Internet is a great resource because it offers an inexpensive way to publish your family history. Before the Internet, many researchers put off publishing their family histories to ensure they had everything about the family identified before committing it to paper and paying to have it printed. Today, you will find many "works in progress" on the Internet. Because they are not etched in stone, it is not unusual to discover upon revisiting a site that the researcher has either changed the pages dramatically or removed them entirely.

You should ask questions about every Web site you visit. The Internet makes it extremely easy to share information, but nothing should be accepted at face value. Make sure to verify the facts before downloading and adding the information to your genealogy program.

DON'T BE SWAYED BY THE PRETTY PICTURES

It's easy to be impressed by the way a Web site looks, especially if it has an elaborate color scheme or lots of graphics, but don't neglect other sites that lack these fancy features. Many genealogists who now share their information online were genealogists long before they knew how to use computers. They may not be familiar with all the bells and whistles available to Web site designers, but that doesn't mean their information is less reliable than what is found on fancier sites.

GENEALOGY WEB SITES: WHERE TO START

You're probably wondering exactly what kind of information is out there. How do beginning genealogists start their search? For genealogists, the Internet is best categorized by types of Web sites, each with its own pluses and minuses.

WHAT'S IT ALL ABOUT?

The Internet contains thousands of Web pages covering every conceivable subject, making it easier than ever to follow the historic path of your ancestors. There are many Web sites devoted to genealogy. Some of them lead you to other sites, and some hold the information you seek. Some are genealogically specific—created with genealogists in mind—while others are general Web sites that can be used for genealogical research.

The Internet is a publishing avenue available to anyone with computer access. Its pages are varied in subject matter, organization, and information. There are many ways to use the Internet—both to identify useful Web sites and to search directly for your ancestors. These include:

- General search engines
- Directories
- Compiled genealogy databases
- Transcribed records
- Compiled family history pages
- Library indexes and catalogs

GENERAL SEARCH ENGINES

If the Internet can be considered a giant library, then search engines are your card catalog to the Internet. Without using the card catalog at your library, it's almost impossible to find the books that will help you. By the same token, if you don't know how to use it effectively, you'll have trouble locating the information you had hoped to discover.

General search engines help people find things on the Internet when they either don't have the Web address or don't know if a site exists for a specific subject. At this time there is no one general search engine that catalogs the entire World Wide Web. There are a number of general search engines, and you may quickly pick a favorite.

General search engines are a catalog of the Internet. Knowing how to effectively use these tools will make your online search more productive.

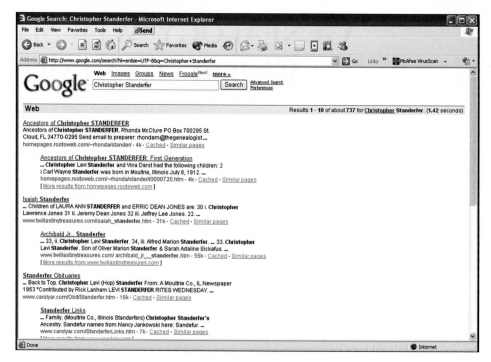

Different methods of cataloguing the Web result in different results from each search engine.

Try these general search engines:
- Google (www.google.com)
- HotBot (www.hotbot.com)
- Dogpile (www.dogpile.com)
- Ask Jeeves (www.aj.com)

Making General Search Engines More Effective

Most genealogists try general search engines for basic research and then dismiss them as their research gets more detailed. This can be a mistake.

No search engine is going to dig up only the information you seek.

NOT *THOSE* DUCKS

There are times when the surname you seek is an actual word, such as *Duck,* for example. Unfortunately, in using general search engines, you'll quickly find that your hits reveal a number of pages about mallards and other breeds of ducks. To avoid such hits, try using a given name. If necessary, use the NOT command. This command tells the search engine to exclude sites that include a particular term. In the Duck example, you might use the following: *Duck NOT mallard.*

False hits are links that lead you to unrelated sites. One way to eliminate possible false hits is to add the word *genealogy* to the search field. Keep in mind, however, that Web sites that don't use the word "genealogy" on the site or encoded in their site will be eliminated from the search results. Be careful that you don't accidentally block useful family history sites with this approach.

Another method is to search for the places where your ancestors lived. For instance, if you're looking for Stephen Webster who lived in Haverhill, Middlesex, Massachusetts, you might try searching for *"Stephen Webster" Haverhill*. This narrows down the number of hits you get and increases the likelihood that they pertain to your ancestor.

Of course, the more common the name, the less effective a general search engine may be. It will take some practice to figure out how to narrow the search without blocking potentially useful sites.

General search engines are also great for digging into the history of an event or locality. For instance, perhaps you've heard a family story about one of your ancestors being buried in Potter's Field in New York City. A general search for *"Potter's Field" New York City* should reveal some sites that detail the history of that particular Potter's Field.

What general search engines cannot do is show you what is contained within the compiled genealogy databases. This is because of the way the data is stored. You must usually use a search tool within the site to view the information.

Never presume that no one else would be interested in the subject you have questions about. The Internet offers the world a place to create pages about their various interests.

DIRECTORIES

Directories offer a different view of the Internet. A directory on the Internet is like an index to a book. A book index tells you the pages on which to find a specific person or subject; an Internet directory tells you the Web sites for a given subject. Whereas general search engines look for terms found either on the

Web page or in the coding (which you don't see but your Internet browser software can interpret), a directory is based on information found on the Web site's home page and is organized with human intervention. Directories are arranged by subject headings, with the list of sites generally organized alphabetically under the subject heading.

Directories can be great time-savers. It's always a good feeling to put the name of an ancestor into a directory and have the name come up. When that happens, viewing the original record is as easy as clicking on the name.

Because of the human involvement, directories may actually give you a better chance of finding pages with genealogical information. There are a number of directories on the Web devoted solely to genealogy Web sites.

Try these genealogy directories:
• Cyndi's List (www.cyndislist.com)
• A Barrel of Genealogy Links (www.genealogytoday.com/barrel)
• Ancestor Quest (www.ancestorquest.com)
• Genealogy Links on the Web (www.genealogy.freewebsitehosting.com)
• FamilyTree.com, A Graphical Genealogy Directory (www.familytree.com)

Q. Is there any way to create searches that you can recall later on, or must you start over each time?

A. If you are using the general search engines described, then yes, you will need to re-create your search each time (another reason to use a research log, so that you can track previous searches). However, there is a search program that allows you to create a search on your computer, after which the program hits all the various search engines for you. To find out more about **Copernic Agent**, visit their Web site (www.copernic.com).

Each directory is arranged differently. The largest is Cyndi's List, with more than two hundred thousand links. She has organized the list into headings and subheadings. For instance, you may select the Newspaper heading, then the History subheading, which contains a number of links to sites on the Internet pertaining to this subject. The organization of the links is up to the people who have compiled the directory. As such, links may not always be under the heading you expect. Some directory sites offer a search function so you can be sure you don't miss any links.

When looking for specific types of data, use general search engines and directories. They help you find databases based on locality, ethnic or religious beliefs, surname, and record type. They may give you an idea of what is out there on the Internet and help you find transcribed records and compiled family history pages.

COMPILED GENEALOGY DATABASES

Raw data is what genealogists hope to find on the Internet. To genealogists, raw data is any name, date, place, or index that will lead a researcher to more records or information. This is why compiled genealogy databases are quickly gaining in popularity.

Some indexes and databases are free of charge, while others are accessible only with a paid subscription. You may be able to jump-start your research by visiting a few of the free databases, and then you may decide to join one or more of the subscription sites later. The free sites allow you to experiment with searches or entering information in search forms. Because these sites are free, you may not feel too frustrated if the search doesn't work right away. Each ancestry is different; the

For newcomers to genealogy and the Internet, directories such as Cyndi's List are a great place to begin family history research.

records and resources that offer the most information differ from researcher to researcher. Using the free sites is a good way to get an idea of whether your particular lineage or the region in which your ancestors lived is one that has been well researched.

Free sites include

- *FamilySearch* (www.family search.org), the Web site of the Family History Library of the Church of Jesus Christ of Latter-day Saints. For anyone who wishes to search for ancestors, this free site includes entries that reveal births, deaths, marriages, family units, pedigrees, ancestors and descendants, and a few indexes to vital (birth, marriage, and death) and census records.
- *Olive Tree Genealogy* (www. olivetreegenealogy.com) offers free databases of ships' passenger lists, some specialty sites for immigrant ancestry, how-to guides, tutorials, and much more.
- *RootsWeb* (www.rootsweb.com), owned by Ancestry.com, is free and has many unique databases that include births, deaths, marriages, military indexes, and databases to keep you in contact with possible relatives. All of these databases have been donated by fellow researchers.

Commercial database sites, such as Ancestry.com and Genealogy.com, offer a large collection of data including indexes, transcribed records, digitized images (which are discussed in the next chapter), and much more. The big question is: Are they worth the price of admission? Most genealogists believe they are if you find what you're looking for, but of

WHERE ARE YOUR ANCESTORS?

Some regions in the United States and the world have been better researched than others, either because more individuals traced their families there or because there were more records available in the early years of genealogy. Some areas, such as New England, England, some parts of Germany, and parts of Canada, have produced many compiled or pedigree databases. Many indexes or methods of accessing the records can be found online.

course there is no guarantee. A rule of thumb with commercial sites is to subscribe for a year, and if during that year you don't find anything, even with the new content added to the collection, reconsider when your subscription is up for renewal. Some subscription sites are available at public libraries, so you may be able to try them there.

Free sites may not be as complete as subscription sites, but their main advantage is, of course, that they are free.

TRANSCRIBED RECORDS

In chapter 2 you learned that a transcript is a typed or handwritten copy of an original document with exactly the same wording, spelling, and punctuation. Records may be

Q. Is there one genealogy site that is better than the others?

A. There is no one site that is best. Good researchers use everything at their disposal. Try out all database sites and other Web sites with genealogical information, and leave no stone unturned: You never know where your ancestors may be hiding.

transcribed from many sources: You'll find indexes and other compiled lists that include vital records, census records, cemetery inscriptions, military records, and more.

Transcribed records were one of the first things to make it onto the Internet, especially with the creation and growth of the USGen-Web (www.usgenweb.org) and the WorldGenWeb (www.worldgen web.org) Projects. These and a number of other Web sites exist solely as a way to share the wonderful volunteer efforts of genealogists around the world. These genealogists transcribe records and put them online, bringing information about a given state, county, town, shire, province, or parish to researchers who may never get the opportunity to visit the courthouses, cemeteries, or other repositories in which the original documents are housed.

Arranged from largest to smallest jurisdiction, these projects include information shared by volunteer managers of the sites. A site may include transcripts of biographies found in county history in the late 1800s as well as indexes to birth, death, or marriage records. You may find that a site offers its members a place to post tombstone inscriptions with or without corresponding photographs of the tombstones in ques-

tion. These sites are also useful for learning the location of original records for a given county or township. Eventually you'll need to use the Internet for more than just looking up names. You'll find that much of its true genealogical wealth lies in helping you uncover what is not available online (see chapter 5).

COMPILED FAMILY HISTORY PAGES

Many researchers have used the *Web page creation* feature in their genealogy program to create a compiled family history page. This refers to narrative-style pages and sites that showcase pedigree charts and family group information on a Web page. You may find that the compiler includes actual pedigree charts and family group sheets in addition to the "story" of the family. Many people who use their genealogy programs to create these pages also have an index, with hotlinks that take you to specific sections of pedigree charts, family group sheets, or narratives.

CHECK IT OUT

Any time you are working with records that have been transcribed by others, there is potential for error. Errors may creep in as the transcriber tries to decipher original handwriting or make out a faded tombstone. These unintentional errors can lead you astray if you don't make a point of verifying the information by checking other resources.

While you read through various charts and narrative reports, making notes and adding information to your own charts, keep in mind that, as with all compiled research, it's possible not all the information is correct. Just as published family histories found on the shelves in many libraries may contain errors, these online versions may also have faults. However, this possibility doesn't mean you shouldn't use the library books or the compiled family histories you find online. In fact, you *should* use them. They point you toward other records that may verify facts or show you errors or discrepancies. They may also provide names of other family members you never knew existed. And every new name you find is one more name for the tree.

Finding these sites requires the use of either general search engines or directories. There are many compiled family history sites containing hundreds of surnames and families. Some sites are devoted to a specific surname; others are the culmination of a genealogist's entire research and include many surnames.

In chapter 3 you were introduced to the idea of citing sources. This is never more important than with sites that contain compiled family histories. Perhaps one of the biggest mistakes researchers make when working with family history pages on the Internet is not going beyond those pages in their research. When you use a compiled family history site, you are viewing someone else's conclusions. In order to understand how accurate these conclusions are, you need to know what records and

BEWARE THE "MY FAMILY" WEB PAGE

You'll find that many genealogists like to name their Web sites "My Family." The problem with this practice is that directories arrange Web sites alphabetically by title, so every "My Family" site is listed under the letter "M." So, when using a directory to find compiled family history Web pages, be sure to check more than just the alphabetical listing for the surname. Look under M for "My Family," T for "The Johnston Family Tree," and so on. Some directories offer a way to search internally for the surnames you're interested in.

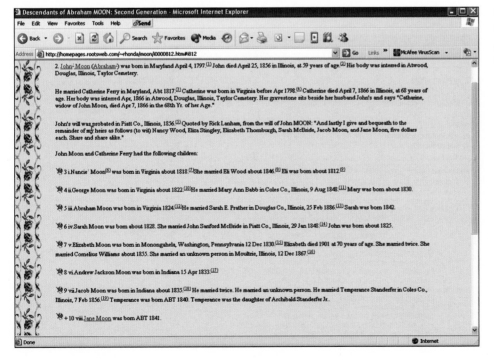

Ideally, each fact should have a source citation, but that doesn't always happen.

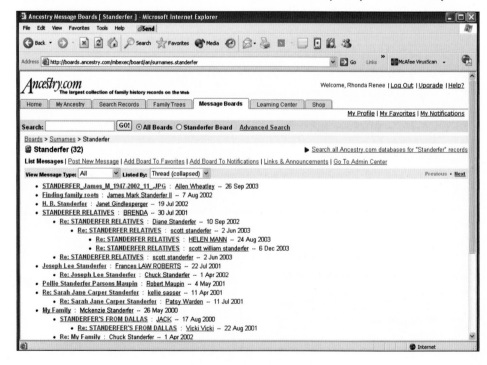

Q. What is the difference between a mailing list and a bulletin board, and how do I find them?

A. The biggest difference between the two is how you access the messages. Mailing list messages, as the name implies, arrive as e-mail messages. Once you've signed up for a specific mailing list, you'll receive messages either one at a time (mail mode) or in batches (digest mode). Each concentrates on a specific subject. On the other hand, to access a bulletin board, you must go to that site to view it, much as you would the bulletin board at your local library.

Bulletin board messages are linked, beginning with the original post and followed by a "tree" of the responses not only to the original post but also to those responses.

© 2000–2004 MyFamily.com, Inc. Screen shot from Ancestry.com.

resources were used. While the information may indeed be accurate, it's important to determine where it came from. Even longtime genealogists make mistakes and, when transferring data to a Web page, may inadvertently mix something up.

If a family Web site doesn't indicate where its information came from, don't hesitate to send an e-mail asking for a source citation. It's not a good idea to ask the Web page manager to share all their records with you, but it is perfectly acceptable to contact them and ask where they discovered their information.

MAILING LISTS AND BULLETIN BOARDS

Family historians also use the speed of the Internet to reach out to people around the world. Mailing lists and bulletin boards provide a convenient way to learn more about genealogy in general and your family history specifically. By the same token, they are a place for you to post messages about your own research, sharing what you've learned and perhaps helping other genealogists in their quest. Along the way, you may even discover distant cousins you never knew you had and find that they are searching for their roots as well. Consider the fact that they may have already discovered the information you are seeking.

There are a number of mailing lists at RootsWeb (www.rootsweb.com). To "subscribe" to these, send an e-mail to the list's "subscribe" address. After signing up, you'll receive messages addressed to everyone who subscribes to the list. Many share data; some are formulated to ask questions. Bulletin boards, on the other hand, are similar to Web pages in that you must visit them to read and post messages. There are a large number of bulletin boards on Ancestry.com (www.ancestry.com/share).

WHERE TO TURN FOR ORIGINAL RECORDS

Recent years have brought online images of certain records frequently used by genealogists. In most instances these records are available only by purchasing a subscription to the company supplying them.

Census records were one of the first offerings of online original records. The census has been taken in the United States every ten years since 1790. Beginning in 1850, everyone in a household was listed by name, along with information regarding sex, age, and place of birth. From 1880 on, relationships of those listed in each household were also included. In subsequent census years, additional information was gathered offering insight into family structure, date of marriage, number of children, occupation, and more.

Because the census lists everyone in a household and in some cases identifies family relationships, it is one of the more popular original records consulted by family historians. You will find many digitized graphics of original records through subscription and free sites.

Subscription Sites
- Ancestry.com (www.ancestry.com)
- Genealogy.com (www.genealogy.com)

Free sites
- USGenWeb Project (www.usgenweb.org)
- Ellis Island Records (www.ellisislandrecords.org)
- HeritageQuest Online (www.heritagequest.com) *available through many public libraries and genealogy societies*

Before looking more deeply into images, one record type needs to be addressed, as it is becoming increasingly digitized: manuscript.

FINDING MANUSCRIPTS

The term *manuscript,* as it applies to records sought in genealogy, refers to any unpublished collection of papers. This could be letters or diaries from someone who traveled the Oregon Trail, for example. It could be the rosters or account books of a general store. It could even be a compiled family history never formally published. The National Union Catalog of Manuscript Collections (NUCMC) (www.loc.gov/coll/nucmc/nucmc. html), is one of the best places to look for manuscript resources. NUCMC's online catalog allows you to search catalog entries from

Q. A.

Why are recent U.S. censuses unavailable?

In the United States there is a 72-year privacy act, a law that prevents federal records such as the census from being released until 72 years after they are taken. Other countries have even longer privacy laws, preventing access for 100 years or more. These privacy laws are designed to keep identifying information sealed until the individuals are deceased, although that does not always end up being the case.

1986 to the present. Pre–1986 entries must be searched in published volumes, which your local public library may have. NUCMC entries include the author (or originator of the collection), the title by which the collection is catalogued, the number of items the collection includes, notes or other important information about the collection, subjects under which it may be catalogued, and the repository housing the manuscript. NUCMC can also point genealogists to repositories with manuscripts available for viewing online.

DIGITIZING RECORDS: THE POWER OF THE IMAGE

Until recently, most of what genealogists found online and used was not original in nature: Indexes, abstracts, transcripts, and compiled family history pages are all the result of human intervention in one form or another. These were either re-keyed from a printed source, run through an optical character recognition program (a program that allows the computer to read and translate into a text the graphic typed letters of a scanned page), or were the result of individuals' conclusions based on their own research.

Original records, such as the census, diaries, rosters, and ledgers, have long been available via microfilm, but until recently were most often located only in the manuscript collections of a single repository. The limited accessibility usually required you to travel to the source or hire a professional researcher to access the records. Today, some of these records are undergoing digitization.

Manuscript collections, such as the New England Historic Genealogical Society's American Revolutionary War pension receipts, are usually a one-of-a-kind collection available in only one repository.

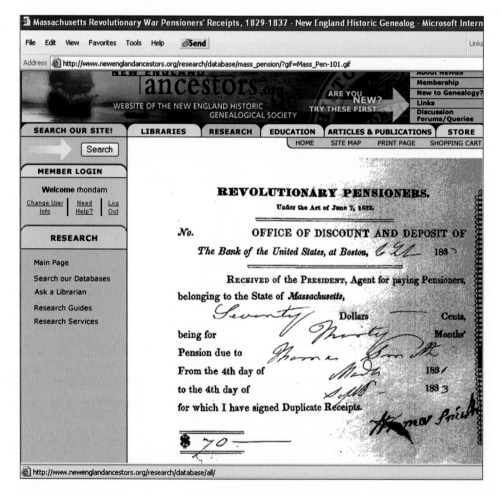

Digitization of records is similar to taking a photocopy or picture of the original document. It means that you are looking at the original page, written in authentic handwriting. For an online record to be considered original, it must be a digitized copy of the record. When working with such a record, you need only worry about the mistakes or shortcomings in the original record, rather than human error during transcription or abstraction.

A census page found online may be considered an original if it is a digitized copy. A digitized copy is the computer equivalent to viewing the census on microfilm. As such, printing a census page from the Internet is just like going to a library, finding that page on microfilm, and making a photocopy.

Of course, digitized files are actually graphics, not text, and they must be downloaded before you can view them. If you don't have a speedy Internet connection, you may find it frustrating to wait for the image to load.

In addition to census records, other items are also being digitized. Complete issues of newspapers, including announcements of births, marriages, deaths, court proceedings, and news items, are a valuable resource in genealogy research.

Genealogists also use passenger lists in an effort to identify their ancestors' native countries and the year or time frame of their arrival in the United States. While only the later passenger lists (those created after 1906) include the actual place of birth, from the 1890s on, records also contain information about relatives left behind, including their addresses. Obviously, this information can be helpful in isolating a

possible place of birth for an immigrant. Perhaps only the head of the family was included in some earlier indexes. Newer indexes of the same records may include everyone in the family unit. Passenger lists are available on microfilm, but not all of them have been indexed. Recent digitization efforts have made some passenger lists available online in index form, so check them out.

Other records that have been digitized include World War I draft registration cards and Civil War pension index cards. Every month brings family historians new resources on the Internet.

Visiting subscription sites and search engines will help you find out what is available. Subscription sites in particular keep subscribers up-to-date on new additions to their sites, usually by posting a message on the front page of the site. They continue to add more records because they want to keep your business.

LIBRARIES GO ONLINE

Some state and national libraries and archives are going a step beyond simply posting their library catalogs online: They are also digitizing some of their more popular collections and making them available online.

The National Archives (NARA) in Washington, D.C., has begun an impressive program called the Access to Archival Databases (AAD) System (www.archives.gov/aad/index.html). This system lets people search and view electronic records. It includes some interesting searchable databases. The National Archives also offers a powerful online inventory of some of the holdings of the main

Q. What types of shortcomings might be found in census records?

A. Census records are not always completely accurate. When the census first started, the enumerator (the individual who went door to door asking the questions that are on the form) was not required to talk to an adult or the head of the household. They could ask their questions of a maid in the house or, if no one was home, they could ask a neighbor. Neighbors may not have known the exact ages or places of birth of the family members, which is why they are sometimes different from one census year to the next.

The Archival Research Catalog (ARC) contains some digital copies of records, but its true value is in showing you the NARA network repository with the record or resource you are interested in.

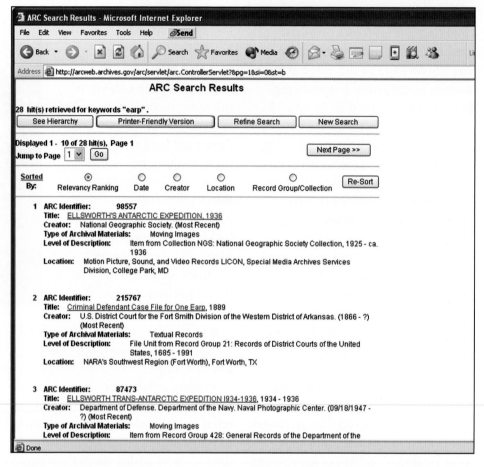

archives in Washington, D.C., as well as their network of 13 regional archives and additional record facilities, through the Archival Research Catalog (ARC) (www.archives.gov/ research_room/arc/index.html). This is far from complete and should not be considered a definitive answer as to whether or not a specific resource is available through the National Archives network.

Many of the regional branch archives have their own Web sites, as do the Presidential libraries. Some of these have their own searchable online catalogs. You can find out more about these repositories by checking out the Locations and Hours link in the Research Room section of the NARA Web site (www.archives.gov).

The Florida State Archives, another repository embracing the

current technology, has digitized a number of its collections, including World War I service cards, Florida Confederate pension application files, and Spanish land grants (some of the earliest records identifying residents in what eventually became Florida).

The online availability of such records is a dream for genealogists. To have such a convenient (and often free!) way to research obscure records is an incredible time-saver. It may save you a trip to the actual repository, but even if it doesn't, it will almost certainly help you accomplish a large portion of your research from home. You can postpone the visit until you have managed to identify other individuals and records needed, in order to make your trip to the archives a truly useful one.

FROM THE INTERNET TO THE LIBRARY... AND BEYOND

Using the Internet is a great way for genealogists to jump-start their research, accruing leads and information even when libraries and archives are closed. Of course, the Internet isn't the only place to find data, so don't stop there. Put your Internet research to work!

ONLINE LIBRARY CATALOGS

Although not all libraries and archives are fully entrenched on the Internet, they remain an excellent resource. Even if you are unable to view original records online, researching a library's archives or card catalog online can be an extremely valuable time-saver. The first step is to use the Internet to uncover existing libraries, especially if the only information you have is the state or county in which your ancestors lived. One way to do this is through a directory of online library catalogs.

LibDex, The Library Index (www.libdex.com), is a great

resource because it shares lists of public libraries, state libraries, law and medical libraries, academic libraries, and more. It allows you to search for libraries using a keyword, such as the city, or a phrase. You can also browse for libraries by county or by state.

LibDex is a list of only those libraries that offer an online site. Not all of these sites will offer online library catalogs, but at the very least the Web site should provide helpful contact information.

Another directory for library catalogs is the Gateway to Library Catalogs (www.loc.gov/z3950/gate way.html). In addition to allowing

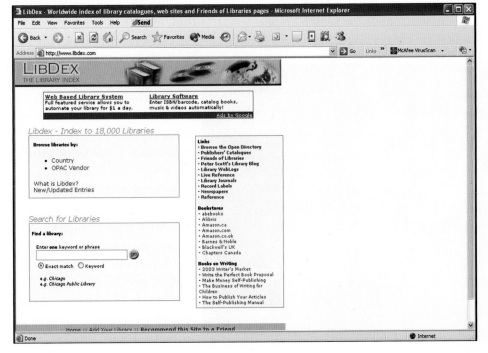

LibDex is a great place to begin when trying to find the libraries available in a given locale.

What is a Soundex search?

A. The Soundex search employed by online databases is a method of indexing like-sounding names together. The index is based on phonetics rather than spelling. A surname is assigned a four-character code derived from the first letter of the surname, followed by three numbers that are based on the additional letters in the surname. Letters with similar sounds are assigned the same number, allowing certain variant spellings to be grouped together. To find out more about Soundex, including the rules on how to code a surname, visit the National Archives' Web page on the Soundex Index (www.archives.gov/research _room/genealogy/census/ soundex.html).

you to search the Library of Congress in Washington, D.C., this site provides a number of links to other catalogs all over the world.

How to Use an Online Index

Indexes that are accessible online require a little different thinking than a printed index. When searching the index to a book, it's easy to evaluate the variant spellings of a surname. For instance, while looking for the surname *Johnson* you may also spot entries for *Johnsen* and *Jonson* and consider checking those out. However, when you type *Johnson* into a computerized index, you will get hits only for this spelling, not for any variations.

Search engines are not designed to guess what might be considered a variant spelling. With the exception of the databases at FamilySearch.org (www.familysearch.org), which group variations together, there are only a few databases that offer an option for alternative spellings. Ancestry.com (www.ancestry.com) allows you to request a *Soundex search*, which tells the search engine to include some variant spellings.

All of the variations for the Johnson surname have the same Soundex code, which means that an online index using a Soundex search would explore these variations and more.

While you don't need to know how to code a surname using the Soundex system when working in online indexes, there are other records for which you will need to figure out the code. Most genealogy programs include a Soundex converter tool, and there are plenty of Web sites that convert names into code for you.

- Free Online Soundex Calculator (www.frontier net.net/~rjacob/soundex. htm)
- Soundex Code Generator in Java Script (www.billcarney. com/brickmasons/genmisc/ soundex.html)
- Surname to Soundex Code (searches.rootsweb.com/ cgi-bin/Genea/soundex.sh)
- Ancestor Search: Surname to Soundex Converter (www. searchforancestors.com/ soundex.html)

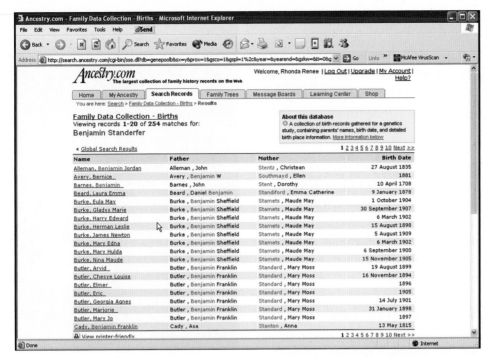

Selecting the Soundex search at Ancestry.com increases your number of hits, though not all of them will be for the surname you are researching.
© 2000–2004 MyFamily.com, Inc. Screen shot from Ancestry.com.

TAKING IT ON THE ROAD

While the Internet may supply a lot of information about your family, especially if you are fortunate enough to locate a detailed compiled family history, it's also important to visit the libraries and repositories that house records not found on the Internet.

To prepare for a visit, check out the library's Web site first. As previously discussed, many libraries have computerized their card catalogs and put them online. This means people are able to search them from home, with their files handy, and map out a plan without having to tote their files all over the place.

The Web site may provide more than just the library's catalog. It will likely list the hours of operation, address, and phone number. Some sites now include driving directions, at least from major highways. All of this is important when deciding when to go and how long to stay. Rules or guidelines and maps of the facility may also be found on the repository's site.

Creating a research log before going to the library is an invaluable time-saver. With it, you can head into the building with a complete list of the resources you plan to check. And by filling out your research log with call numbers and other details ahead of time, you can immediately begin your research when you get to the library. Remember to fill in your log as you complete your research, making notes about both positive and negative results.

Most libraries or archives, especially those of genealogical interest, have special holdings of one-of-a-kind manuscripts or resources that are old and deteriorating. As a

WHERE ARE THEY?

If you don't find your ancestor in the index, do not automatically presume he or she is not listed in the actual records. If all your research indicates that your ancestor should be there, it might be necessary to scour the actual records rather than rely on the index. Sometimes a name has been misindexed or overlooked during the indexing process.

Many of the libraries frequented by genealogists are privately owned specialty libraries, as opposed to public libraries that are supported by tax dollars. Donations, entry fees, and registration fees are some of the ways in which private libraries raise money to keep the library going and to preserve and restore the records genealogists and researchers use.

result, they have to institute certain rules to protect their collections. For instance, some repositories restrict what visitors can bring into the research room. Some allow the use of notebook computers; some don't. Some allow pens and notebooks; others don't. This is important to know before you get there, because you'll want to be well equipped. If computers are permitted, arm yourself ahead of time by uploading your genealogy database, the program that runs it, and your research logs.

WHAT KIND OF LIBRARY?

Before becoming interested in family history, you may not have thought very much about different libraries. You may have visited your local public library to complete a school project or to check out a book to read, but you may not know what else is available. Genealogists use different types of libraries for various purposes.

If you have been searching the NUCMC catalog, you may now have a list of specialty libraries to visit or obtain records from. Spe-

cialty libraries include any library devoted to a region, an occupation, a religion, and more. Some specialty libraries are devoted to genealogy, such as the Family History Library in Salt Lake City, Utah, and the New England Historic Genealogical Society in Boston, Massachusetts.

Libraries differ in how they allow access to their resources. Some, in an effort to better control and protect their unique collections, rely on a "closed stack" approach. This means that you must fill out a request form in order to use a book in the collection. Checking the online library catalog is all the more important in these instances, since it usually takes some time for the technicians or pages to pull the volumes you request. Other libraries keep their books on open shelves, where researchers may peruse the different volumes available.

It's also a good idea to ask about photocopying when you visit a library or other specialty repository for the first time. Some libraries will let you make your own photocopies,

BRINGING THE RESOURCES TO YOU

Even though the Family History Library is located in Salt Lake City, genealogists still have access to a large part of its collection locally. Family History Centers (FHC) are located all over the world. They are usually found in local chapels of the Church of Jesus Christ of Latter-day Saints, but they are open to anyone interested in researching their family history. FHC personnel will assist you in using their resources—whatever your religion. Through your local FHC, you may also request copies of microfilm to be shipped from Salt Lake City; you'll only pay the cost of shipping.

Similarly, members of the New England Historic Genealogical Society may lend some of their books for a short period of time. The society will mail them to you for a small shipping fee.

while others make them for you. This is often determined by the library's responsibility for the records in their possession. Some have collections for which they must monitor all photocopying. Other collections are stamped with a warning so that you cannot reproduce it yourself—perhaps because of a copyright issue or an agreement with the original donator of the records.

Public Libraries Many large public libraries house genealogy departments. Usually these departments are comprised of some basic genealogy resources, with much of the collection devoted to records and books about the local area or area residents. But just because your ancestors did not live in a certain locale, don't presume that the local library won't be of use to you. For instance, the Orlando Public Library offers a large collection of records devoted to New England, which may seem strange until you consider the fact

that many "snowbirds"—those who travel south from the northern states—spend their winters in the Central Florida area.

Small community public libraries may not have a section devoted to genealogy. That doesn't mean they won't be useful, however. At a small library, try asking the librarian what information they have about the history of the community, including their newspaper archives. There's plenty of genealogical information to be found in even the smallest of libraries.

State Libraries State libraries are usually directed to the preservation of records applying to the state in question. Using the library's online catalog gives you insight into the holdings of the state library. You may discover that it houses a large collection of state newspapers or a manuscript collection of papers for industrial titans for that state.

University Libraries University libraries do not usually have a genealogy department, but they

Q Why is it so important to make copies of the records you find? If you've seen the information and added it to the database or charts, why keep a copy?

A. No matter what you find or where you find it, if you can get a copy of it, do. As you progress in your research, you may discover dates or places that conflict with information you've already recorded. Having a copy of each record allows you to judge for yourself which is more accurate, based on when the record was created and who created it.

which is devoted to genealogy for the world (see page 42). Another library of note is the Newberry Library in Chicago, Illinois. Though not a genealogy library, it has a comprehensive collection of local and family history. Their collection contains records from the United States and Canada, though its most extensive information concerns the Midwest. There is also a sizable British Isles collection.

Use the Entire Library

Though you may go to a library with a specific purpose in mind, don't forget to take a little time to see what else is available. Just as different libraries offer varying resources, other departments may provide additional and equally useful books or records. Consider a local public library in a community to which you've traced your ancestors. You may find city directories or other volumes that provide insight into their lives.

City directories may not only reveal your ancestor's name in the

Q. Is there any library or repository that wouldn't contain records of genealogical value?

A. In a word—no. Family history is the study of an ancestor's life. Records of your ancestor's life can be found in any number of places. The best researchers do not dismiss any possibilities. Being creative not only in the records you look for, but also in the places you search, extends the scope of your research. The wider you cast your net, the more chances you have of finding a treasure.

have a history department and much more. These libraries can be extremely useful for looking at county histories and manuscript collections, as well as other unique historical, rather than genealogical, records and collections. These records may provide a wealth of information about your family.

Yearbooks, alumni books, and newsletters are also stored in university libraries. You might find your ancestor in a yearbook, helping you estimate a date of birth. Alumni newsletters often list former students who have died, giving you valuable information including maiden and married names for women. If the deceased was active within the alumni association, you may discover that the newsletter contains more information about him or her than an obituary.

Specialty Libraries Specialty libraries offer their own benefits. You have already been introduced to the Family History Library,

film, may be found in the library's audio-visual department. If you fail to investigate beyond the usual avenues, you may not learn as much as you could have from your visit.

alphabetical listing of the inhabitants of a city, but may also include a "reverse index" that lists by house number those who lived on a given street. This provides a look at the names of neighbors—names you may recognize within the family you are researching. City directories also provide information about churches, organizations, and associations. Your ancestor may have attended one of those churches or been a member of one or more of the groups. If nothing else, you are being exposed to additional avenues of research.

City directories are usually published the year after the actual information was collected. This means your ancestor, who gave information in 1919, may have moved by the time the directory appeared in 1920. The ability to identify when your ancestor arrived in and left a city is a bonus to your research and may help you fill in the years between census records.

Biographies or histories of the growth of a state, county, town, or region may not be found in the genealogy department, but rather in the history or social history section of a library. Newspapers and other periodicals published long ago, because they are stored on micro-

There Must Be More

As you spend time in the library, you'll get a feel for other records that can be useful to you. Within compiled family histories, for example, you'll find a wide variety of records mentioned in the sources they cite.

You'll want to see what else a library's shelves have to offer, and find out what types of indexes or abstracts to land records, wills, estate files, court records, and newspapers have been published by genealogical societies or individual genealogists. If you are at a large library devoted to genealogy, such as the Family History Library, it may be possible for you to go from the published index or abstracts to the original records. Other times, in order to get the records, you may

Reliving History

At first it might seem easier to cut to the chase and concentrate solely on the names, dates, and places that will help you fill in the gaps in your genealogy chart, but in the long run you'll discover it helps to unearth more than just the cold hard facts about the people you're researching. Your search is likely to be more rewarding and interesting for it—you'll realize that understanding the history your ancestors lived is essential to understanding the decisions they made.

Q. What can you do when a tombstone has begun to deteriorate and is no longer easily readable?

A. In the past it was common to spray shaving cream on the tombstone and use a squeegee to "fill in" the etching on the stone to make it more visible. Other times genealogists took rubbings, which required taping a large piece of paper to the tombstone and rubbing a soft wax crayon over it. The lifted impression provided a good view of the etched words. However, both of these methods are now discouraged. The chemicals in shaving cream and the pressure of crayons can damage the stones, causing them to deteriorate more quickly. Instead, try using the sun to your advantage. Instead of taking a picture straight on, shift to one side or the other before snapping the picture. You may be able to see the words more clearly this way. Using mirrors to redirect the sunlight is another approach. And if you have a digital camera, you may be able to manipulate the image once you upload it to your computer to increase the contrast and bring out the words and numbers.

need to travel to the original source, write a letter requesting a copy of the records, or hire a professional to access them for you. Many researchers consider this phase of the research the real detective work.

THE DETECTIVE IN YOU

Genealogy can be a never-ending mystery. Consider that every time you uncover a new answer, such as the parents of a previous generation, and enter the information in your pedigree chart, you are immediately presented with a new question: What can you find out about both of *their* parents? The further back you trace your pedigree, the more separate lineages you discover, with ever more questions to answer. Thus you are always on the trail of clues, putting your deductive reasoning skills to the test.

While it is true that a lot can be accomplished now without leaving the comfort of your home, some of the real adventure comes when you visit the homes of your ancestors. Suddenly history comes alive, and you want to find out even more about them. Remember, the best family historians leave no stone unturned, taking the clues that they have and following up on them.

So, take what you find online and verify it with original records, ideally those with primary information. These may be available on

microfilm, accessible through your local public library or Family History Center, or may require a road trip to the family homestead.

CEMETERIES

You'll know you've become a full-fledged family historian when you find yourself planning family vacations around the towns where your families lived and died. You'll find yourself looking forward to visiting the cemetery and taking pictures of the tombstones.

For genealogists, cemeteries hold many valuable clues. Tombstones

DON'T GIVE UP

Too many of today's researchers presume that if they cannot find something on the Internet, it doesn't exist. There are millions of records that have not made it onto the Internet yet, so chances are the information you seek *does* exist—you just need to look somewhere else to find it. Experienced family historians know that the challenge of following clues out into the field is part of the fun.

contain information about your ancestor's life, including the name and some indication of when that person lived and died. But tombstones hold much more than just the names and dates. If you look to see what else has been etched into the stone, sometimes you'll find a Bible verse or elaborate carvings of praying hands, angels, or small animals. Other times you'll be rewarded with insignias representing organizations or military involvement.

Friends and Neighbors Another benefit of a personal visit to the cemetery is seeing who is buried near your ancestors. They are often related in some way. You may discover children who were born and died between census years. You may find leads for a woman's parents. You may stumble upon spouses of children for whom you had been unable to locate a marriage record. Many things can be found in the cemetery and in the communities in which your ancestors lived.

WHERE'S MY GREAT-GREAT-GRANDMOTHER?

Perhaps because over the course of history women have changed their surnames throughout their lives (from maiden names to one or more married names), it can be more difficult to trace a woman's lineage than a man's. This is especially true of family histories of the late 1800s and early 1900s. The compilers of such histories ignored the descendants of the female children in each line. As a result, researching women often requires a little ingenuity.

Getting death certificates for all the children of your great-great-grandmother may help you identify

CAN'T VISIT THE CEMETERY YOURSELF?

There are a couple of interesting Web sites that have become quite popular for genealogists. Find-a-Grave (www.findagrave.com) and the Virtual Cemetery at Genealogy.com (www.genealogy.com/vcem_welcome.html) offer an opportunity to view a tombstone online. Armed with digital cameras and small notebooks, fellow researchers visit cemeteries in their area, take pictures, and write down any information available. They upload the images and the information onto the Internet, making them freely available to other researchers.

her maiden name. Often the death certificate of one child does not contain all the information, perhaps because the informant did not know it; another child's records may provide more facts.

Also, try looking for her husband's land and court records; these may reveal some surnames to investigate more thoroughly. It's possible her husband bought or sold land to or from her father or brothers. Seldom

daughter is often mentioned in the will with her married name; in the estate papers, her husband may have been required to sign receipts or other records.

These are only a few ways to identify a woman's maiden name. You may also find information from another researcher in one of the various online compiled databases. Of course, visiting the communities where your female ancestors lived gives you perhaps the best opportunity to identify their maiden names. Tombstones often include maiden names, or you may find that your ancestors are buried in a family plot under a surname you have not previously encountered.

In the local libraries of smaller communities you may be able to read through newspapers of long ago. These libraries may even have collections of information on citizens who have passed on. It never hurts to investigate what a library or small courthouse has to offer. Churches may also share their archives or older records. Much of

will that relationship be included in the land record, but if you see the record of a land sale for an interestingly low price, say $1, it's a good idea to investigate the seller more thoroughly. Many times a new son-in-law was given land after the marriage.

If the couple in question married after 1850, census records might help verify the connection between the wife and the seller of the land. You may look for the seller's family in the census to see if there is a female child with the right name and appropriate age. Remember that all your finds coming before 1880 are supposition, since the census did not list relationships until then. However, if you do find such a child, you may search for a will or an estate file for the seller to see if the woman is mentioned. If they were married before the will was written or the estate was probated (when the personal and real property was dispersed to the heirs), the

this type of research should be done in person, as you may not get a positive response if you contact these groups by post or e-mail. In person they may help you by pointing you to the records and letting you go through them, but if you contact them by mail, they have to do all the searching, and they may not be willing to do that.

GIVE ME MORE RECORDS

The records listed in these pages are the ones used most frequently. Most may be found online, making it easier to begin your research. But there are times when you must turn off the computer and turn your attention to other, undigitized, records. For a brief checklist of records and the types of information you may hope to find in them, see page 50.

Different records supply different pieces of the puzzle, and when put together, they provide a fuller picture of your ancestor's life. As you

progress in your research, you'll recognize the need to find records that are unique to the particular county, state, province, or country of your ancestors.

COURTS, CRIMINALS, AND CORONERS

Some of our ancestors didn't appreciate the fact that we would eventually want to locate them. Some spent a great deal of effort avoiding the census taker, for instance. When you find that your ancestor is not in the census records, or that vital records were not being kept at the time your ancestor was living in the county, it's time to consider what other records might give you the missing information. You may consider looking for court records and coroners' reports.

Certainly not all of your ancestors were criminals or scofflaws, and maybe none of them were, but many people are surprised at some of the legal issues our ancestors faced. Consider the many "blue laws" (extremely stern laws that were enacted in an effort to regulate morals and behavior) enforced in Colonial times. At one time, a woman could be taken to court for yelling at her husband, for example. There may be records of such transgressions.

Court records include a variety of trial actions and decisions. Some are the simple types we see today—for instance, a dispute over the boundary between two neighbors. Some are the result of disagreements in

INFORMATION YOU CAN FIND IN RECORDS

Record	Information Likely to be Found
Birth record	Full name of the child; date of birth; place of birth; names of parents (including maiden name of mother); ages of parents at the time of the birth; state or country of birth of the parents
Marriage record	Full names of the groom and bride; age at the time of the marriage application; place of birth; how many marriages each has had; date and place of the marriage; name and office of the individual who performed the marriage; parents' names
Death record	Full name of the deceased; date and place of death; cause of death; marital status; date and place of burial; age at time of death; date of birth; place of birth; names of parents (including maiden name of mother); places of birth of the parents
Will	Name of the testator (the author of the will); date written; names of relatives, usually with relationships identified; indications of property ownership; date the will was produced in court for probating (thus giving you an idea of when the testator died)
Land record	Name of the individual buying or selling the land; in the case of a land sale, the given name of the wife; the land description; to whom it was sold or from whom it was bought; the amount of money that changed hands; names of neighbors whose land bordered the described property
Census record	After 1850 in the United States, the name and age of everyone in the household at the time of the enumeration; state or country of birth; occupation; literacy; and health issues. Beginning in 1880, census includes relationships, place of birth of parents, naturalization information, and more
Naturalization records	Name of the individual being naturalized; date or approximate time of arrival; the name of the ship upon which they arrived; dates and places of filed records that make up the naturalization process; names of spouse and children, with ages or dates and places of birth; date and place of birth of the immigrant
Tombstones	Name of the deceased (sometimes with the maiden name of the woman); date of death; places of birth and death; names of parents; insignia or other information to identify occupation or fraternal affiliation
Newspapers	Almost anything, from announcements of birth, marriage, or death; outcome of legal trials (divorce, suits, etc.); memorials with biographical information; write-ups about anniversary celebrations; and more

the probating of an estate. Other times the situation is more serious, when someone committed a crime, for instance. Don't dismiss the search for court records because you are afraid of what you might find. For most people there will be few surprises, but the unexpected events you do find may help you in your search. Court trial records usually include witness testimony that can identify how or how long the witness knew the accused. There may be indications as to when your ancestor arrived in the county or town. Additionally, if bail was posted, you may find relatives put up the bond money for your ancestor, giving you new names to research as you continue the quest.

Your ancestor did not even have to be accused of anything in order for court records to be of value to you. You may find material from the details shared in a deposition for a suit or in the answers to an interro-gation during a trial, if your ancestor was the plaintiff in an action or a witness.

There are different types of courts, from county level to district level to federal level. A good place to begin looking is at the local county level. So, as with many other records, including vital, land, and probate, you'll need to contact the clerk of the court at the courthouse.

Coroners There are many reasons why a coroner is required to investigate a death. Murders and violent and/or unexplained deaths may require investigation under county or state laws. You may presume that there are no useful details for your research other than how the individual died, but most inquests include witness and other testimony from which a few helpful tidbits may be gleaned.

Coroners' records are harder to access than court records, as they

You never know how much information you may find in court records.

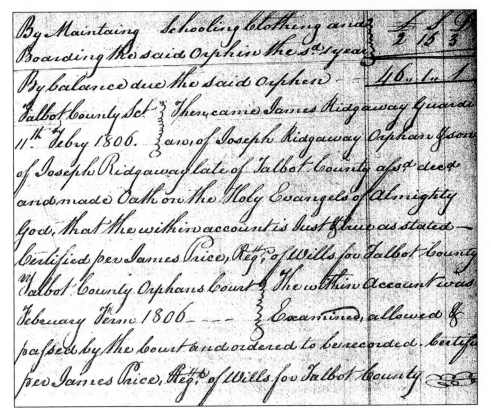

are not as likely to be microfilmed or available long distance. You may need to contact the local coroner's office to see where their records are housed for preservation. To find out how to contact the county or city coroner's office, access a phone book for that area. You may also find such phone numbers online through the various county sites.

MILITARY RECORDS

As you research, especially as you read county histories, you may find that many of the men in the community were in the military. Some of those wars were fought on home soil, while others took the men, and some women, far away.

Many military records are now located at the National Archives, to which you were introduced earlier (see page 37). Some of these records are on microfilm, but most of them are still filed away in folders.

For earlier wars, such as the American Revolution, the War of 1812, and the Civil War, there may be two types of military records. The first is the *service record,* which details the mustering date and pay the individual received. It offers some information about the units in which the soldier served and the location in which he was stationed. It may indicate if he was sick or captured. The other record, which usually includes more of the genealogically pertinent facts we crave, is the *pension record.* Pension records consist of proof of marriage, births of children, and date and location of the deaths of soldiers or veterans.

YOU ARE NOT ALONE

As you venture into libraries and Family History Centers, you'll meet other genealogists. You may wonder where or how they learned to use records or find things you have not been able to find. Talk to them! Ask them about local genealogical societies that offer seminars and guest speakers who are experts in the field. There's always something new to learn and someone willing to teach you.

Bow-Tie Style Pedigree Chart

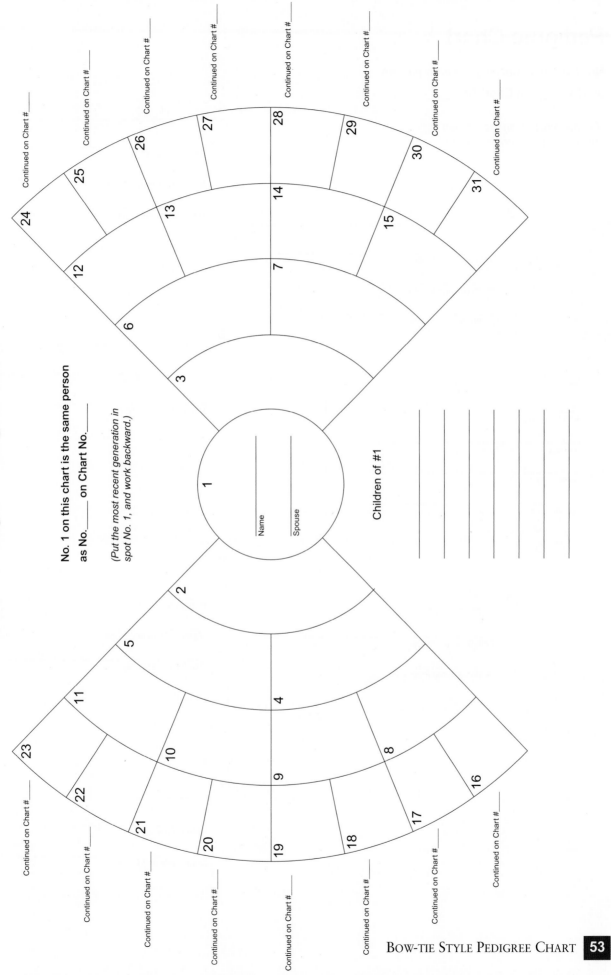

No. 1 on this chart is the same person
as No. _____ on Chart No. _____

*(Put the most recent generation in
spot No. 1, and work backward.)*

1

Name

Spouse

Children of #1

2
3
4
5
6
7

8
9
10
11
12
13
14
15

16
17
18
19
20
21
22
23
24
25
26
27
28
29
30
31

Continued on Chart # _____ (×16)

Pedigree Chart

No. 1 on this chart is the same person
as No._____ on Chart No._____

*(Put the most recent generation in
spot No. 1, and work backward.)*

4

Birth Date and Place

Marriage Date and Place

Death Date and Place

2

Birth Date and Place

Marriage Date and Place

Death Date and Place

5

Birth Date and Place

Death Date and Place

1

Birth Date and Place

Marriage Date and Place

Death Date and Place

Spouse

6

Birth Date and Place

Marriage Date and Place

Death Date and Place

3

Birth Date and Place

Death Date and Place

7

Birth Date and Place

Death Date and Place

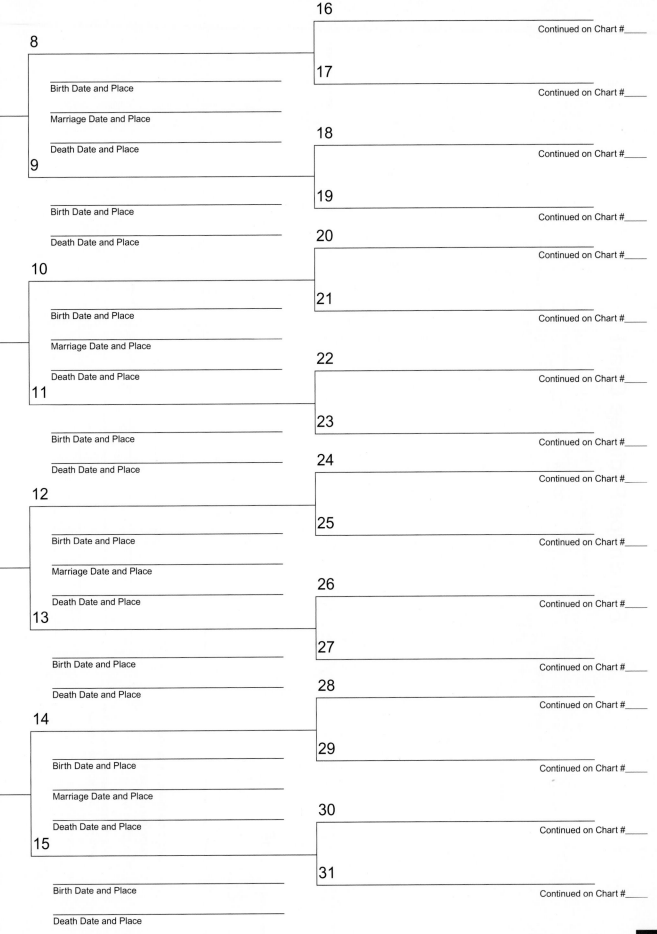

8

Birth Date and Place

Marriage Date and Place

Death Date and Place

9

Birth Date and Place

Death Date and Place

10

Birth Date and Place

Marriage Date and Place

Death Date and Place

11

Birth Date and Place

Death Date and Place

12

Birth Date and Place

Marriage Date and Place

Death Date and Place

13

Birth Date and Place

Death Date and Place

14

Birth Date and Place

Marriage Date and Place

Death Date and Place

15

Birth Date and Place

Death Date and Place

16

Continued on Chart #_____

17

Continued on Chart #_____

18

Continued on Chart #_____

19

Continued on Chart #_____

20

Continued on Chart #_____

21

Continued on Chart #_____

22

Continued on Chart #_____

23

Continued on Chart #_____

24

Continued on Chart #_____

25

Continued on Chart #_____

26

Continued on Chart #_____

27

Continued on Chart #_____

28

Continued on Chart #_____

29

Continued on Chart #_____

30

Continued on Chart #_____

31

Continued on Chart #_____

PEDIGREE CHART **55**

Fan-Shape Pedigree Chart

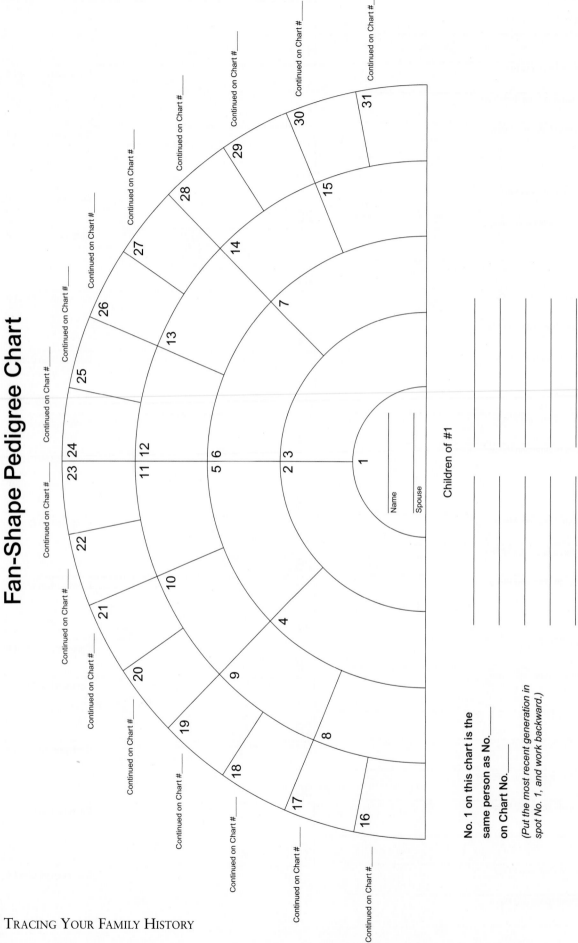

Name _____

Spouse _____

Children of #1

_____

_____

_____

_____

_____

**No. 1 on this chart is the
same person as No. _____
on Chart No. _____**

*(Put the most recent generation in
spot No. 1, and work backward.)*

Continued on Chart # _____

Research Log

Researcher _____

Subject Name(s) _____

Locality

Time Period

Search Date	Location/Call #	Description of Source (Title/Author/Publisher/Year/Page #)	Notes

Census Check _____
Name

Date of Birth/Place of Birth _____   First Census _____

Father's Name _____   Mother's Name _____

Date of Marriage/Place _____   Spouse _____

Date of Death/Place _____   Burial Place _____

Census Year	Age	State/Counties Searched	County Where Found/Notes	Film #, Roll #, E.D., Pg. #

Notes

GLOSSARY

Abstract: the recording of pertinent facts from a given record.

Ancestors: those individuals from whom you descend—your parents, grandparents, great-grandparents, and so on.

Ancestral file: a lineage-linked database of families submitted by fellow researchers and available online to search at the FamilySearch Web site (www.familysearch.org).

Census: the enumeration of the population by the government. Used to, among other things, adjust boundaries or representation in the government; identify the number of citizens who may be used in fighting; determine the number of immigrants to the country.

City directory: the precursor to phone books. An alphabetical listing of inhabitants of a city in a given year, supplying the addresses of individuals, providing meeting information about various organizations and churches, and identifying businesses in the community.

Civil registration: the records of births, marriages, and deaths (more commonly referred to as *vital records*).

DAR: Daughters of the American Revolution, a lineage society that requires proof of descent from an ancestor who either fought for or gave aid to the Colonial army during the American Revolution.

Derivative source: any source or record that is not an original source; that is, anything that has been compiled, copied, or abstracted and is being used as a source.

Descendants: those individuals who descend from someone. You are your parents' descendant; your children and grandchildren are your descendants.

End-of-line ancestor: the last individual of a given line you have been able to identify.

Family group record: the chart or form that allows you to record information about a single family unit, which includes the father, mother, and children.

Family History Center (FHC): a local branch of the Family History Library in Salt Lake City, Utah. Provides access to more than two million reels of microfilmed records. Look in the yellow pages under Latter-day Saints (Mormons) or

Church of Jesus Christ of Latter-day Saints to find your local FHC, or use the "Find a Center" link at the FamilySearch Web site (www.family search.org).

Family tradition: in family history, the stories and traditions passed down from generation to generation.

Gazetteer: a dictionary for places. Supplies details such as the county in which a town is located, the names of nearby towns and rivers, and sometimes the population of the town at the time of publication.

GEDCOM: acronym for GEnea-logical Data COMmunication, a method of transferring information from one genealogy program into another without having to reenter it manually.

Genealogy: the recording of the ancestry or descendants of a certain individual.

Homestead records: land records generated when an individual received land, usually 160 acres, under the Homestead Act of 1862.

Inscription: refers to the informa-tion that appears on a tombstone, ranging from the deceased's name and year of death to elaborate bio-graphical information including date and place of birth, organiza-tions to which the person belonged, name of parents, and more.

Interpretation of records: the infer-ences and assumptions based on the records found.

Land platting: a graphical represen-tation of the land description found in a land deed or patent.

NGSQ style: a narrative-style genealogy report used by the National Genealogical Society Quarterly. Adheres to a numbering system that assigns a consecutive number to each individ-ual and identifies the descendants who had issue (had children) by adding a plus mark (+) next to their number.

Lineage-linked: refers to genealogy databases in which the individuals are connected through family rela-tionships and can be displayed in pedigrees and family groups.

Manuscript: any group of papers with a common theme or topic compiled by or created around an individual or family. May include letters, diaries, and other private papers or notes.

Original source: a source created at or near the time of the event by someone who was present or knowledgeable about the event.

Parish: a term used to describe either an ecclesiastical (church) or civil government division. Also, in the state of Louisiana, counties are referred to as parishes.

Pedigree chart: a chart that has been referred to as the road map of your ancestry. Also known as the *family tree,* as each new generation adds more branches to the chart.

PERSI: acronym for the PERiodical Source Index, compiled by the Allen County Public Library in Fort Wayne, Indiana, and indexing periodicals that contain genealogical information.

Primary information: written or oral information supplied by someone who was present at the event in question, either as a participant or as an eyewitness.

Presidential libraries: those libraries established to preserve the papers of past presidents of the United States after they leave office, beginning with the 31st president, Herbert Hoover, and continuing to the present.

Register style: a narrative-style genealogy report that adheres to a numbering system in which each descendant of the primary individual is assigned a consecutive number; children are assigned lowercase Roman numerals as well as Arabic numbers.

Repository: any building that holds records or resources for safekeeping. Includes archives, libraries, museums, society buildings, and businesses.

Research log: a chart or method of tracking research, including the research you have already acquired and that which you intend to obtain.

SASE: a self-addressed, stamped envelope, which researchers should include any time they contact a repository, family member, or fellow researcher via postal mail with a request that they respond.

Secondary information: any statements, written or oral, from a person who was not present at the event in question. Includes family traditions and stories along with many other types of information.

Soundex: an index based on phonetics, with consonants being assigned one of six numbers, and the surname being converted to a four-character code.

Source citation: a notation that identifies the exact location of the information you are including on a family group sheet or in a genealogy program database. Can include, but is not limited to, books; land, census, or vital records; tombstones; newspapers.

Vital records: certificates recorded by civil authorities to identify births, marriages, and deaths (also known as *civil registration*).

INDEX